"The reality of God's love f[
to dawn upon us, particul[
past and present failures. In such moments, it seems impossible to
us that the Father could love us. Dan Cruver is right.

So, how do we come to truly know that we are loved indeed?
Dan takes a fresh look at Paul's letter to the Ephesians to help
Christians in a cosmic struggle to believe the truth of the gospel.
He teaches us how to experience the fullness of the Father's love.
The enemy of our faith is a liar. Christ has died to take away our
sins and bring us to the Father. When you read Dan's book, you
will be assured of the Father's eternal commendation: 'This is my
beloved Son, with whom I am well pleased.'"

John Fonville, Rector, Paramount Church, Jacksonville, Florida,
and author, *Hope & Holiness: How the Gospel Enables and Empowers Sexual Purity*

"Every pastor, counsellor, and individual who has struggled with
knowing and experiencing the love of God should read this book!
There are a lot of books that explain God's love and what we can
do for assurance, but this one is unique. Dan Cruver shows how
our experience of God's love is an intense spiritual battle that we
all face. This book won't leave you feeling guilty for not sensing
God's love or give you a to-do list to experience it. It won't give
you new strategies or quick fixes. It will give you gospel hope in
the work of God in the person of Christ. It will usher you into
resting in the finished work God has done for you and his simple
yet mysterious infinite love for you!"

Jason Kovacs, Executive Director of Gospel Care Collective

"Dan Cruver has given us a balm for the aching soul. Whether you are plagued with guilt, doubt, anxious thoughts, or insecurity, you'll find encouragement from the Scriptures to know deep down that you are loved indeed by the One who made and can heal your heart."

Catherine Claire Larson, author, *As We Forgive: Stories of Reconciliation from Rwanda*

"'How do I know I am saved? I don't feel that God loves me—how do I know he does? Does he even care I exist?'

Sadly, these are questions that many Christians struggle with daily but are too afraid to tell anyone about. The shame that comes with such doubts crushes the minds and hearts of believers. From his own experience, Dan Cruver sits down with the reader and points him chapter by chapter to the gospel. God's love for us, not our love for him, produces joy and confidence. Whether you have been following Christ for five days or fifty years, this book will bring comfort to your heart because it reminds you of how amazing God's love is towards you."

Jon Moffitt, Pastor, Grace Reformed Church, Spring Hill, Tennessee, and cohost of the weekly podcast Theocast

"Because we are flesh and blood—and because we are sinners— we tend to be suspicious of God and his love for us. We are prone to view him as harsh, angry, exacting, and threatening. It is even possible for us to twist the work of Christ and think that Jesus has had to convince the Father to reluctantly save us. But that is the design of the Evil One, not God.

So, what do we need? To be regularly reminded of God's love

for us. That he smiles on us and rejoices over us. That he delights to save us. That the triune God has planned from all eternity that Jesus would accomplish everything we need for salvation. In this excellent book, Dan Cruver leads us to the unchanging love of God for us, our resting place."

Justin Perdue, Pastor, Covenant Baptist Church, Asheville, North Carolina

"A glorious, living application of Ephesians to the suffering and insecurities of this life. Dan Cruver has given us solid ground to stand on when the waves of life make everything feel unstable. A vulnerable, vivid, honest, biblical, comforting, and hopeful vision of life in a painful world. It's all here in this short book of divine comfort."

Tony Reinke, author, *12 Ways Your Phone Is Changing You*

"'Does God really love me?' Dan Cruver is refreshingly honest about the question so many of us are afraid to ask out loud. And rather than simply giving us his own reassurance, he points us to the Scriptures and reassures our hearts of the very heart of God for us.

I was incredibly blessed by this book. Dan's willingness to share his amazing and heartfelt story of how he discovered the love of God gives us faith that we might experience this reality as well."

Laura Story, Executive Director of Worship, Perimeter Church, Atlanta, Georgia

LOVED INDEED

Reassurance for the Doubting and Suspicious

Dan Cruver

Union
Publishing

CONTENTS

To my wife of 32 years.

Melissa, you have loved me because
the Father first loved you in Christ.
Together, in sickness and in health, we
have leaned into the objective reality of
our Father's love for us in his Son,
by the presence of his Spirit.
I dedicate this book to you because it is
a joy to love you and be loved by you.

ACKNOWLEDGEMENTS

Special thanks to Michael Reeves, who encouraged me to write this book. I would not have written it had you not done so.

Many thanks to the saints at Heritage Bible Church in Greer, SC. First, to the students in our high school and college ministries, who were the first to hear the substance of this book and received it joyfully. Second, to Trent, for encouraging me to preach this as a two-part series to the entire congregation. Third, to Joel Frans and Tom Mackintosh, for reading the original versions of these chapters. You men encouraged me more than you know. Thank you, Heritage.

A very special thanks is due to Eleanor Trotter. You are a gifted and brilliant editor. *Loved Indeed* would not exist without you. In many ways, you taught me to write in a way I didn't know I was capable of.

ACKNOWLEDGEMENTS

I'm also grateful for Rebecca Rine, senior editor at Union Publishing. Your ability to see through the eyes of my readers is really quite remarkable.

Years and years of thanks to my brothers, Stephen and David. We have reminded each other of the Father's love, to the praise of his glorious grace, through laughter and tears. I am proud to call you my (younger) brothers.

Finally, with all of my heart, I would like to thank my wife, Melissa, and my children, Hannah, Isaiah, and Noah. You all have loved me indeed for decades now. What a gift it is to be loved by each of you.

FOREWORD

Sinclair B. Ferguson

It is an honour to introduce Dan Cruver's *Loved Indeed*. It tells a story that will sometimes move you, perhaps occasionally surprise you, and undoubtedly encourage you. I do not mean to spoil your own reading of it by explaining in detail why this is likely to be so; but perhaps a few reflections will underline that the value of these pages is far greater than their number.

You will find it *moving* for the simple reason that it tells the story of severe trials. That in itself will draw you in to listen to a voice that speaks from deep experience of God's ways and the discovery of his light and grace.

You may find it *surprising* because of the unostentatious honesty with which Dan Cruver writes. And then perhaps also by the way in which some of his own story, even if quite different from yours, resonates deeply with you. For like him, one of our greatest needs is to be able to discover with King David, "in your light do we see light" (Ps. 36:9).

You will find it *encouraging* because while God providentially shapes each Christian's life differently, he has the same goal in view for all of us. It is that we might be "conformed to the image of his Son, in order that he might be the firstborn among many brothers" (Rom. 8:29). There is much to be learned from Dan Cruver's tracing this pattern in his own life and reflecting on it.

Reading *Loved Indeed* reminds us that the Christian life is a perpetual battle. All of us have been caught up in the conflict inaugurated as long ago as Genesis 3:15—a verse that runs like a river through the whole of the Bible. But Dan Cruver's story has also reminded me of some of the principles enshrined in God's love for us that the saints in every age have had to learn.

It reminds me of the "Joseph principle," that God's love is unhurried. He spent fourteen long years shaping an impetuous seventeen-year-old teenager into a thirty-year-old man with the wisdom and patience to handle the strains and stresses of the next fourteen years of plenty and famine intimated in Pharaoh's dreams. And in his love, God made Joseph an agent of grace to bring reconciliation to both his brothers and their father. His sore trials were in fact the investment of divine love (Gen. 45:5–7; 50:20).

These pages are also a reminder of the "Peter principle," that God's love looks to our future. I am thinking here of Jesus' words to Peter when he resisted the Saviour kneeling to wash his feet: "What I am doing you do not understand now, but afterward you will understand" (John 13:7). For there is a "now" and also an "afterward" in each of our lives. Trials "now" often grieve us because we cannot see if or how they will have any significance "afterward." But as Peter came to see, tested faith is more precious than gold and "afterward" results "in praise and glory and honor at the revelation of Jesus Christ" (1 Pet. 1:7).

And then, *Loved Indeed* is also a reminder of the "William Cowper principle," and of how John Newton's much-tried poet friend was led through dark valleys to trust in the sovereign love of a heavenly Father:

> God moves in a mysterious way
> His wonders to perform;
> He plants his footsteps in the sea
> And rides upon the storm.

Cowper's words are an echo of Psalm 77:19. Footprints planted in the sea cannot be seen. But as biblically instructed poets like Cowper and authors like Dan Cruver share their lives with us, they give us glimpses of the way God walks. They teach us how to recognise his steps:

> Deep in unfathomable mines
> Of never-failing skill;
> He treasures up his bright designs,
> And works his sovereign will.

And we also learn from them this lesson:

> Judge not the Lord by feeble sense,
> But trust him for his grace;
> Behind a frowning providence
> He hides a smiling face.

Of course, the great question is: how can we be so sure that the hiding face is still smiling on us? How can we learn to trust him when we encounter "tribulation, or distress, or persecution, or famine, or nakedness, or danger, or sword" (Rom. 8:35)?

How can we find *love indeed* then? Dan Cruver found it. More accurately, it found him. Indeed, his story is itself an echo of Cowper's testimony:

The bud may have a bitter taste,
But sweet will be the flower.[1]

But I must leave Dan himself to tell you this story—his story—of how, and where, *Love Indeed* can be found. I feel sure it will be a help to you.

Sinclair B. Ferguson

---

1   William Cowper, "God Moves in a Mysterious Way" (1774).

INTRODUCTION

*From the Prodigal's Suspicion
to Loved Indeed*

For as long as I can remember, I have struggled with a tendency towards severe introspection and doubt in just about every area of life. Although I can't recall a time when I didn't believe in Jesus, even as a young child I was plagued with doubts that my faith wasn't sincere enough. As I entered my teenage years, I'd often look inwards at my faith, my repentance, my love for the Lord, and begin to question all of it. *Is my internal spiritual world genuine? Do I really love the Lord, or do I just think I do? And, will I one day hear the words: "I never knew you; depart from me"*[1]?

These thoughts were paralyzing. I was regularly unnerved by what was going on in my internal world.

I've sat across the table from enough Christians to know that I am not alone in this kind of struggle. As I've talked with fellow

1   See Matthew 7:21–23.

strugglers over the years, I've seen tears run down their faces. It's more common than you may think for believers to share these thoughts and feelings. Doubts are not unusual in a life that is lived by faith, not by sight (2 Cor. 5:7). So, take heart, for if this is your struggle, you are not, and never have been, alone.

What we also have in common is the desire for reassurance and a fresh experience of God as our exceeding joy (Ps. 43:4). This is the desire of every saint who has ever lived.

In my twenties, I learned how to suppress my troubling thoughts somewhat, just to survive. Of course, they were always there, hiding in the background like a lion crouched in the sub-Saharan bush ready to pounce, but at least I could function relatively normally. In God's kindness, during those years I learned to look more steadily at the immutable object of my faith, Jesus, rather than at my changeable internal world.

That was a real step forwards, because to seek assurance by looking at one's faith is a losing endeavour. It ends up being an "assurance by faith in *faith*" instead of "assurance by faith in *Christ*." Just as "we do not lay hold of our salvation by faith in faith" but "only by faith in Christ,"[2] so also we only deepen our assurance by looking not at our faith but at Christ. That central truth enabled me to hold my paralyzing doubts at bay.

But something was still missing.

My confidence that I was right with God the judge grew as I learned to look more steadily at Christ and what he had done for me in his life and death. But in spite of this growing assurance that God had declared me righteous through faith in Christ, I still lacked a genuine sense that the Father loved and

2   Graeme Goldsworthy, *The Goldsworthy Trilogy* (Wheaton, IL: Crossway, 2000), 170.

cared for me *personally*. As a result, I would still sometimes question whether or not I was truly right with God the judge. If the love of the Father was like the sun, then the light of his love had not yet dawned in my heart. So, while I was no longer as often terrified by the darkness of doubt, I had yet to experience the daily assurance of God's love. And that was a problem. The theologian J. I. Packer wrote, "To be right with God the judge is a great thing, but to be loved and cared for by God the Father is a greater."[3]

If you share something of my struggles, you may well ask, "When did everything begin to change?" Everything changed one day when I read the following insight from the Scottish theologian Sinclair Ferguson:

Although [the parable of the prodigal son] is probably the best known and loved of all Christ's parables, the lesson it teaches us *as Christians* is often overlooked. Jesus was underlining the fact that—despite assumptions to the contrary—the reality of the love of God for us is often the last thing in the world to dawn upon us. As we fix our eyes upon ourselves, our past failures, our present guilt, it seems impossible to us that the Father could love us.

Many Christians go through much of their life with the prodigal's suspicion. Their concentration is upon their sin and failure; all their thoughts are introspective. That is why (in the Greek text) John's statement about the Father's love begins with a word calling us to lift up our eyes from ourselves and take a long look at what God had

3   J. I. Packer, *Knowing God* (Downers Grove, IL: InterVarsity Press, 1973), 188.

done: Behold!—look and see—the love the Father has lavished upon us![4]

It was a lightbulb moment.

The phrase that most arrested my attention was "the prodigal's suspicion." *That's it!* It finally occurred to me that even though I was now mostly confident that God had declared me righteous because Christ's righteousness was counted as mine, I was still very aware (sometimes painfully so) of my imperfect faith, past failures, and present guilt. As a result, if you had asked me if I thought God loved me, I would have said yes. But what I did not know was the *warmth* of his love. *Does his love for me ever move him towards me in tenderness, or is his love more "tough love" than wooing love?*

I had no trouble at all in seeing warmth and delight in the Father's love for his eternal Son. After all, on a number of occasions, Scripture goes out of its way to allow us to overhear exactly how the Father feels about his Son:

And behold, a voice from heaven said, "This is my beloved Son, with whom I am well pleased." (Matt. 3:17)

And a voice came from heaven, "You are my beloved Son; with you I am well pleased." (Mark 1:11)

And a cloud overshadowed them, and a voice came out of the cloud, "This is my beloved Son; listen to him." (Mark 9:7)

---

4   Sinclair Ferguson, *Children of the Living God* (Edinburgh; The Banner of Truth Trust, 1989), 27 (emphasis original). See 1 John 3:1.

And the Holy Spirit descended on him in bodily form, like a dove; and a voice came from heaven, "You are my beloved Son; with you I am well pleased." (Luke 3:22)

For … he received honor and glory from God the Father, and the voice was borne to him by the Majestic Glory, "This is my beloved Son, with whom I am well pleased." (2 Pet. 1:17)

Yet as wonderful as those verses are, my trouble was that I couldn't imagine the Father ever saying such things about *me.*

The solution that Ferguson offered me was quite simple: stop looking inside myself, at my own subjective evaluation of whether or not the Father delights in me. Rather, look outside of myself, to the objective love of the Father that was revealed in, and lavished on me by, his Son. In order to experience *subjectively* the love of the Father, I didn't need to keep searching for some kind of internal feeling or perception that I could hope was there but could never really verify. Instead, God was inviting me to look at his *objective* love, as shown in his giving of his Son for me.

Believe me, I know just how difficult it is to stop looking within, as doing so can feel like ignoring the problem altogether. My car has a faulty engine light that I've had inspected several times, and despite learning that it tends to stay on for no valid reason, ignoring it always seems like a real mistake—negligence, even. *What if there is an actual problem with the engine this time?* However, for Christians, what is of utmost importance is not how we feel, but what Scripture reveals. While our subjective internal world is often misinformed, God's Word is always true.

And that's where this book comes in. It will assist you in experiencing the Father's love by turning your attention away from yourself and focusing it instead on the Son's life, death, resurrection, and ascension—all of which were objectively accomplished for you. And as this happens, you will feel the warmth of God's love in your heart afresh.

However—and this is important to note—if you are someone who tends to look inwards at your spiritual coldness instead of outwards at the warmth of the Father's lavish love for you in Christ, there is so much more at work than the makeup of your temperament. Sure, your personality may be more introspective than you would like it to be. But there are also external forces ever at work to convince you that the Father could never love you with infinite delight. In other words, you're in the midst of a battle, and the battle isn't only with yourself. Evil forces are dead set on keeping you from feeling the warmth of God's love. And the only way to counter those forces effectively is to rely on Christ.

Let's take a closer look at the battle that rages against you. I pray that you will understand more fully what is going on and that, increasingly, you will be convinced that you are *loved indeed*.

PART 1

Our Battle and
Our Strength

1

OUR BATTLE

One of the darkest nights of my soul began on a late-night flight home from Ethiopia in January 2008. I was returning from visiting an orphanage in Shashamane, a town about five hours south of the Ethiopian capital, Addis Ababa.

I have visited many countries and encountered much spiritual darkness. But never have I felt what I can only describe as demonic oppression as intensely as I experienced it on that trip.

On every one of the six flights that it took to get home, I struggled profoundly with what I have just shared in the Introduction: personally experiencing God's love. With great ease, it seemed, the Evil One was building against me what seemed like an ironclad case.[1] Or, to change the metaphor, it almost felt as if he had me in his jaws and would not let me go.

---

1 Scripture identifies the "Evil One" as Satan or the devil (Matt. 13:19; John 17:15; Eph. 6:16). He is an adversary who relentlessly labors to deceive and ravage us as God's image bearers (John 8:44; 1 Pet. 5:8).

I was already familiar with my vulnerability in this area, yet every time I attempted to rehearse the gospel to myself, quoting text after text of Scripture as I flew over the darkness of Africa, I found no help, no encouragement.[2] I had been robbed of every vestige of comfort, and I felt utterly powerless to do anything about it. During those many lonely hours in the black sky, my powerlessness felt increasingly like hopelessness.

Six flights of physically debilitating doubt would have been bad enough, but each also included something I had never experienced before: a panic attack. It was as though my physical symptoms were matching my internal sense of hopelessness. Adrenaline pumped through my body almost the entire thirty-six hours it took to travel home. And the day after I landed, I came down with a 102-degree fever. This went on for seven days, with the fever hovering between 101 and 103.

David's words eloquently describe the kind of effect that the intensity of this struggle had upon me: "I am in distress; my eye is *wasted* from grief; *my soul and my body also*" (Ps. 31:9, emphasis added). That trip was a battle. Not only in the sense that it was a terrible struggle to endure, but in that evil spiritual forces seemed to have aligned themselves against me in a coordinated and sustained attack. I was not merely wrestling against my own sin, weakness, and unbelief, but against a spiritual enemy determined to devour me.

Sabotaged versus seeing and savouring

This battle that waged against me was, in short, a battle for love.

---

2   I share more detail about this experience and how God met me in it in chapter 3 of Dan Cruver, ed., *Reclaiming Adoption: Missional Living through the Rediscovery of Abba Father* (Minneapolis, MN: Cruciform Press, 2011), 33–48.

Not so much for my love for God, either to win or to steal it, but a ruthless battle *against* the Father's love for me: with the aim that I would never again know it, enjoy it, or rest in it.

As I have shared my experience with other believers over the years, I have come to realize that this type of struggle is all too common among Christians (1 Cor. 10:13). Yet the adversary who wages this war against us seeks to isolate us and make us feel like we are fighting all alone: he wants us to believe that our struggles are unique and that no one else can understand what we are going through.

This couldn't be further from the truth. Others suffer too, as we know. And no matter what we are facing, we can take comfort in the fact that God is with us always (Deut. 31:6). It is therefore absolutely crucial that we resist the enemy's lies and cling to the truth of God's Word.

As the great Puritan John Owen wrote, our enemy knows that "God must be revealed unto us as lovely and desirable, as a fit and suitable object unto the soul to set up its rest upon, *before we can bear any love unto him.*"[3] If Satan can prevent us from seeing and savouring the desirable and wonderful love of the Father for us,[4] he knows he will sabotage any expression of our love for our Father in return. So, if you are convinced the Father doesn't love you, then, naturally, there is no way you will ever love him back. If you don't actively run from him, then you will at least avoid him.

Have you ever found yourself avoiding God, even when you

---

3 John Owen, *Communion with the Triune God* (Wheaton, IL: Crossway, 2007), 120, emphasis added.

4 To understand the importance of seeing and savouring, read John Piper's *Seeing and Savoring Jesus Christ* (Wheaton, IL: Crossway, 2004).

knew you really should seek him out? Perhaps you were convinced that God didn't love you, and as a result you kept your distance. The truth is that God loves you with an everlasting love (Jer. 31:3), and he desires to reveal himself to you as a lovely and desirable object for your soul to rest upon.

No book in the Bible speaks more directly about the battle for love, as I like to call it, than Paul's letter to the Ephesians. This book is unique in its ability to shed light on the importance of understanding and experiencing the transformative love of the Father. In the first three chapters, Paul emphasizes the Father's love for us and the significance of our relationship with him. This understanding is crucial to our ability to love him in return, a topic Paul addresses in the final three chapters. This teaching has been a lifeline to me.

Unfortunately, our enemy understands all too well the significance of this battle, so much so that he will do anything in his power to prevent us from experiencing the Father's transformative love. He knows that if he can rob us of the realities detailed in the first half of Ephesians, we will be unable to "walk in a manner worthy of the calling to which [we] have been called" (4:1). In other words, if the enemy can prevent us from understanding and experiencing the Father's love, then he can prevent us from living a life of Christian purpose and fulfillment. It's that serious!

Are you tired of feeling that resting in the Father's love is a constant battle? You don't have to fight alone, for in this letter to the Ephesians, Paul provides us with the tools we need to overcome the struggle and experience true, transformative love. By immersing ourselves in God's Word and meditating on the Father's unconditional love for us, we can equip ourselves to love him back and live lives of purpose and joy. Trust me, this journey is worth taking, and I'll be there to cheer you on!

A battle—really?

At this point, you may be wondering if a battle is really being waged against you. *Of course it's a battle*, you may think, *in that I often find myself struggling to believe that the Father loves me. But is it really a battle against me by some cosmic power? That seems too … well, too cosmically fantastical to be true. Isn't my struggle due more to my own sin and weakness than to the schemes of the devil? Isn't blaming the Evil One just a way to make excuses?*

I'm certainly not saying here that our sin and unbelief have nothing to do with our struggle. And, speaking personally, my sin and unbelief do indeed work against me in this battle. They are not my allies any more than your sin and unbelief are yours. Your spiritual failures are problems—big ones, as are mine.

But there is much more going on in this struggle than just what is wrong with you. Paul's point at the end of Ephesians is that there are evil spiritual forces ever working to use your spiritual failures against you:

Finally, be strong in the Lord and in the strength of his might. Put on the whole armor of God, *that you may be able to stand against the schemes of the devil.* For we do not wrestle against flesh and blood, but against the rulers, against the authorities, *against the cosmic powers over this present darkness, against the spiritual forces of evil in the heavenly places.* Therefore take up the whole armor of God, *that you may be able to withstand in the evil day,* and having done all, to stand firm. Stand therefore, having fastened on the belt of truth, and having put on the breastplate of righteousness, and, as shoes for your feet, having put on the readiness given by the gospel of peace. In all circumstances take up the shield of faith, with which you can extinguish all *the flaming darts of the evil one*; and take the helmet of salvation, and the sword of the Spirit, which is the word of God, praying at all times in the Spirit, with all prayer and supplication. To that end, keep alert with all perseverance, making supplication for all the saints, and also for me, that words may be given to me in opening my mouth boldly to proclaim the mystery of the gospel, for which I am an ambassador in chains, that I may declare it boldly, as I ought to speak. (Eph. 6:10–20, emphasis added)

So, as you can see, the war for your soul isn't just an internal struggle between your passions and God's truth. There is a much bigger spiritual battle being waged by the devil and his minions. Paul speaks of cosmic powers that seek to undermine your relationship with God. The devil is a cunning adversary, always ready to exploit your weaknesses and sins to keep you from experiencing the fullness of the Father's love for you.

We noted earlier John Owen's appreciation of the significance of the battle for love. He was not ignorant of the Evil One's hellish schemes against you, schemes designed to make you doubt God:

Flesh and blood is apt to have very hard thoughts of [the Father]—to think he is always angry, yea, implacable; that it is not for poor creatures to draw nigh to him … Now, there is not anything … more subservient to the design of Satan upon the soul, than such thoughts as these. Satan claps his hands (if I may say so) when he can take up the soul with such thoughts of God: he has enough—all that he does desire.

Satan sows the seeds of fear and tricks you into thinking it is presumptuous to believe what God himself has told you:

> Men are afraid to have good thoughts of God. They think it a boldness to eye God as good, gracious, tender, kind, loving … Is this not soul-deceit from Satan? Was it not his design from the beginning to inject such thoughts of God?

And what response to such deceit does Owen propose?

> Assure thyself, then, there is nothing more acceptable unto the Father than for us to keep our hearts unto him as the eternal fountain of all that rich grace which flows out to sinners in the blood of Jesus.[5]

Hope in your battle

Encouragingly, in the midst of this, Paul's main concern for us in Ephesians is to enable us to "be strong in the Lord and in the strength of his might" (6:10).

By now, you may be starting to realize more fully that many

---

5   John Owen, *Communion with the Triune God* (Wheaton, IL: Crossway, 2007), 126–28.

of your doubts and suspicions about the Father's loving disposition towards you owe their existence to "spiritual forces of evil in the heavenly places" (v. 12). Once I began to realize that myself, I began to feel hope again, for if the devil is ever working to make us doubt the Father's love for us, and if God has already provided a way for us to defeat those doubts, then we have every reason to feel hope again. Right now. At this very moment.

As we delve deeper into the topic of spiritual warfare and the doubts that may arise in our minds, note the rich words from the opening of Ephesians reminding us of the incredible spiritual blessings that are ours in Christ. Allow these truths to sink in and renew your hope and confidence in the Father's unending love for you:

> Blessed be the God and Father of our Lord Jesus Christ, who has blessed us in Christ with every spiritual blessing in the heavenly places, even as he chose us in him before the foundation of the world, that we should be holy and blameless before him. In love he predestined us for adoption to himself as sons through Jesus Christ, according to the purpose of his will, *to the praise of his glorious grace*, with which he has blessed us in the Beloved. In him we have redemption through his blood, the forgiveness of our trespasses, according to the riches of his grace, which he lavished upon us, in all wisdom and insight making known to us the mystery of his will, according to his purpose, which he set forth in Christ as a plan for the fullness of time, to unite all things in him, things in heaven and things on earth.

In him we have obtained an inheritance, having been

predestined according to the purpose of him who works all things according to the counsel of his will, so that we who were the first to hope in Christ might be *to the praise of his glory*. In him you also, when you heard the word of truth, the gospel of your salvation, and believed in him, were sealed with the promised Holy Spirit, who is the guarantee of our inheritance until we acquire possession of it, *to the praise of his glory*. (Eph. 1:3–14, emphasis added)

Everything your Father has done for you was done "to the praise of his glorious grace" (v. 6) or "to the praise of his glory" (vv. 12, 14). The Father's ultimate purpose was to bring glory and honor to his name—that was his intention in lavishing all the riches of his grace upon you (v. 8).

But you may be wondering at this point what "to the praise of his glorious grace" actually looks like in your experience. How do you know when you are praising the Father's great grace, as he intends for you to do?

Awe and wonder

As he shares what the Father has done to reveal his lavish love for you, Paul intends this opening section of Ephesians to cause your heart to go, "Father, the fact that you have loved me in Christ before the foundation of the world is astounding news. What love! You did all this for *me*?"

When that happens in your heart, you are praising the Father's glorious grace: *What, Father, you love me like that? How can it be? What lavish grace!*

The letter to the Ephesians begins with the Father's intentions (ch. 1) and concludes with the devil's (ch. 6). Your Father intends you to enjoy the worship-filled and joy-overflowing assurance of his love for you. He wants you to rest and rejoice in his love. By contrast, your enemy intends that you live in doubt and suspicion. He wants you to crumble under the weight of it all.

One of my favourite singer-songwriters is Laura Story. She is able to write songs that are at the same time theologically rooted and deeply personal. Many of these are inspired by her own experiences and struggles, and they draw you in with their strong focus on faith, hope, and joy in the good news of the gospel.

I attended one of Laura's concerts some time ago, and she told us the moving story of her husband Martin's battle with a brain tumour about a year or so after they got married. Before surgery, the neurosurgeon told them that Martin might wake up after surgery not remembering anything about his life. Not his parents. Not her. Not anyone. Terrifying!

The day of Martin's surgery arrives. After long hours of waiting and wondering, he is finally taken to recovery. When Laura walks in, she wonders if Martin will remember her. But to her great surprise, as she later recalls, "As soon as our eyes met, he said, 'You're Laura Story.' And I thought, 'Oh, good; he remembers me.' And then I could tell he was a little confused, and he said, 'What are you doing here?'"[6]

Yes, Martin remembered her, but not as his wife. He knew she was the well-known singer-songwriter and childhood friend, but he had no idea that they were married. "Laura," he

---

6   Laura and Martin Story share this account in a two-part podcast hosted by Focus on the Family Broadcast, "Finding Unexpected Blessings in Marriage" (April 11 and 12, 2017).

exclaimed, "you came to see *me*?" The thought that such a special person had come to visit him filled him with awe and wonder.

That's something of what we are to feel as we meditate upon Paul's opening words in Ephesians. God, who made us, loves us. God, who owns all things (Deut. 10:14–15), chose us. And he sent his Son to save us and his Spirit to indwell us. God, who rules the universe, came to see us. He came to see *you*. Laura's song "O Love of God" seeks to evoke that same kind of awe and wonder within us by inviting us to contemplate the fact that God does indeed love us—not because we deserve it, but because he gives us his love as a free gift:

> O love of God, strong and true,
> In my barren soul a river running through.
> O love of God, swift and straight,
> You have washed away my sin and leave no trace.
> River, rise and carry me away
> I see You in the stars above
> I feel You in the earth below
> In waves that swell, in winds that blow
> I marvel at the mystery
> That One so great could love someone like me
> Undeserved and free
> O love of God
> O love of God[7]

7   "O Love of God." Writer credits: Cindy Morgan, Ian Cron, and Laura Story. © 2013 Checkpointchicky Music (BMI) / Seems Like Music (BMI) / Brownie Hawkeye Music (BMI) (all admin. by BMG Rights Mgmt. c/o Music Services) / New Spring Publishing (ASCAP) / Laura Stories (ASCAP). All rights for the world on behalf of Laura Stories admin. by New Spring Publishing. All rights reserved.

This is the great truth that the Evil One wants you to doubt. Resist him! How very kind and gracious of the Father to give you a letter like Ephesians so that you are strengthened for those times when this struggle rages. You are *loved indeed.*

So, how do you prepare yourself for those dark times in your life? That's what we will now consider.

2

OUR ARMOUR

In 1999, my wife Melissa gave birth to our second child, Daniel William Cruver II. The pregnancy was normal. All Melissa's prenatal check-ups went well. We had no reason to believe that our boy would not be born a healthy baby.

But thirteen hours after his birth, he suffered what looked like a seizure. I called for our nurse, but before we could process what was happening, Daniel was in the Neonatal Intensive Care Unit (NICU). What began as a single seizure soon turned into ten, then fifty, then one hundred.

After a week in the NICU, the hospital sent Daniel home with us, along with two seizure medications. We were thrilled to have him home, but still a dark cloud loomed: the doctors did not know what was causing the seizures. Within just a few weeks, Daniel was suffering anything from forty to seventy of them a day. No matter what we tried, no combination of medications would even touch his symptoms. Daniel's life was one of constant suffering.

If you have ever had to watch a loved one suffer, my heart goes out to you. The pain and sadness can be overwhelming. Feelings of helplessness interspersed with flashes of despair can be difficult to put into words. And beyond those struggles, it's easy to feel like nobody understands what you're going through. I've been there. And if you're there right now, I pray that the Father will graciously meet you as you read, and that you may feel more hope than you've yet known.

Fast-forward three years. Daniel turned three on Saturday, October 12, 2002. Even though his seizures remained unrelenting, it was a wonderful day of celebration, with my entire family giving thanks to God for this wonderful little boy. We laughed. We cried tears of gratitude. But the very next day, in our church's parking lot, disaster struck: Daniel stopped breathing. My wife administered CPR as I sprinted to find someone to call 911. Fortunately, by the time the emergency vehicles arrived on the scene, Daniel was breathing again. Relief all round.

But that relief did not last. After two days in hospital, Daniel was sent home on an apnea monitor, only to end up in the hospital again a few days later. This pattern was repeated two more times.

After that third time, our doctors told us the devastating news no parent ever wants to hear: our precious little Daniel would never leave the hospital again.

It was truly ghastly. But God was so very kind to us in those final weeks. Time and time again, he met us in the Scriptures when we needed it most.

I remember sitting alone in Daniel's NICU room late one night, feeling utterly overwhelmed. My Bible was in my lap, but

I couldn't even make the simple decision of what to read. So I decided to let my Bible fall open and read wherever my eyes landed.[1] The words that entered my heart through my eyes at that moment were: "Surely he has borne our griefs and carried our sorrows" (Isa. 53:4). It was exactly what my broken heart needed to hear. Jesus, the Son of God, had borne my grief. The Lord was strengthening me with his personal presence through his comforting Word.

I felt the Lord's presence more intensely for a while. In fact, I felt it right up until the excruciating moment when, days later, Daniel took his final breath. But mere seconds after his heart stopped beating, suddenly I felt abandoned and alone. I remember wondering, *Why would the Lord strengthen me with his comforting presence in the days leading up to Daniel's death only to leave me alone at the crucial moment of his death?* I just couldn't make sense of it.

As we saw in the previous chapter, the Evil One ever schemes to use our trials against us and destroy our confidence that the Father is always for us. He knows that if he can get us to be suspicious of the Father, then he can prevent our hearts from expressing praise for the Father's glorious grace. But thankfully, God did not leave me in that condition very long.

Our Father is not ignorant of the devil's schemes. Of course not. So he does not leave us on our own to stumble around in dark times, simply telling us to grin and bear it or tough it out. Rather, he has lovingly provided us with customized armour. Let's now zoom in further on Ephesians and focus on our vital means of protection in the battle: our armour.

---

1   This is not my normal practice, so I do not typically recommend it. This occasion was an exception because I found it difficult to think clearly under the weight of such a burden.

Paul writes, "Put on the whole armor of God, that you may be able to stand against the schemes of the devil" (6:11). Our purpose in this book is not to provide an exposition of every piece of armour; we will focus solely on those three that have explicit connections with earlier parts of Ephesians:

- "the belt of truth" (v. 14)
- "the gospel of peace" (v. 15)

and

- "the shield of faith" (v. 16).

The belt of truth

When you are tempted to believe that your Father does not love you, or that he merely tolerates you, or that he sometimes abandons you when you need him most, what you need to hear most is truth.

Often when I read the word "truth," I can hear Jack Nicholson's character in the 1992 movie *A Few Good Men* yelling from the witness stand, "You can't handle the truth!"[2] But that's the direct opposite of what Paul is thinking here: he knows that we can't handle the devil's lies. Your Father knows that you will not be able to bear up under these lies unless he provides you with the one truth that can shine light into the darkness of the Evil One's deception.

When Paul writes, "Stand therefore, having fastened on the belt of truth" (6:14), he is not talking about truth in general, or even truth that is found in Scripture as a whole (e.g., 2 Sam. 7:28; Ps. 119:160; John 17:17). Rather, this is a particular truth

---

2   *A Few Good Men*, directed by Rob Reiner (Columbia Pictures, 1992).

claim that speaks directly to the lie that the Father has not set his love upon you, but rather merely tolerates you.

Earlier on, Paul had written, "In [Christ] you also, when you heard the word of truth, the gospel of your salvation, and believed in him, were sealed with the promised Holy Spirit" (Eph. 1:13). So, Paul tells us straight up what he means by "truth." If there is one truth that can drive away the dark evil of the devil's deception, it's the truth revealed in the gospel: "the gospel of your salvation."

Bear with me a moment. We noted in the previous chapter how Paul opened the passage containing verse 13 above with these heart-stabilizing words: "Blessed be the God and Father of our Lord Jesus Christ, who has blessed us in Christ with every spiritual blessing in the heavenly places" (1:3). Everything from verse 3 down to verse 14 details what the Father has done to bless you in Christ. So, when you get to "the word of truth, the gospel of your salvation" in verse 13, this surely means the gospel message of what your Father has done in Christ to accomplish your salvation.

That gospel says to you: *Look at all the love the Father has lavished upon you* (v. 8). *He has spared no expense to bring you to himself* (v. 7). *The Father loved you long before you were even aware of him* (v. 4). *He loved you even when you were his enemy* (2:1–3). *So, why would he ever stop loving you now?*

This is the very gospel that Paul directs our gaze to in chapter 6, when he calls us to put on "the belt of truth." The cultural context is significant. In first-century Israel, people wore long, flowing robes. So, the person needing to engage in combat would cinch up his robe with a belt so that he would not fall at his enemy's feet by tripping over his own clothes.

The key to resisting the devil is to rest in the truth that God's gracious love has been revealed through Christ, giving you full access to the Father. Always remember the comforting words of Ephesians 2:18: "For through [Christ] we both have access in one Spirit to the Father." That's not only good news about your salvation, but also the protective news you are to use against your cosmic enemy. This knowledge of your access will keep you standing on your feet. Until Christ returns to finally and fully judge the devil, we will always need this "belt of truth."

What does this look like in practice? It often involves prayer: crying out to God even when our feelings or our mind tell us that he is absent or that he doesn't care. Regularly reading or listening to Scripture will also keep God's revealed truth at the forefront of our minds. And as wonderful as it is to remind ourselves daily of all the Father has done for us, we also need people around us who will readily do that for us too. When my confidence that the Father loves me is attacked, I usually need more than my own voice reminding me of the truth of the gospel. Thankfully, in God's kind providence, I have a wife and close friends who are very quick to add their voices to the chorus of good news.

So, in the light of our need to have more voices than our own speaking truth to us, may I suggest that you invite a few key people to read this book with you after you finish it? These can be family members, trusted friends, or even a small group from your church. Reading and discussing the contents together can serve as a means of reinforcing the truth of the gospel as you remind each other of the love and grace of our heavenly Father. Furthermore, this can provide a welcome space for encouragement as you strive together to live in the light of this truth.

Never doubt

Come back with me to the hospital on that unforgettable October day in 2002. When the light of the Father's love was being sucked out of my heart into the black hole of darkest doubt in the hours following my son's death, I needed words more than anything else. Yes, words.

Now picture another scene, a fictional one this time. Imagine that as my wife and I were leaving the hospital that day, the Apostle Paul was sitting in the lobby near the exit. Noticing us exhausted, grief-stricken, with tears streaming down our faces, Paul knows all too well how the Evil One loves to leverage suffering and will gladly exploit the devastation of our heartbreak to tempt us to think that the Father is against us. He is deeply aware that the Evil One wants to reframe our loss to us so that we begin to doubt: *Do you recall those times when you were so worn out from having to hold your son day after day, week after week, month after month while he suffered seizures that you eventually laid him down in his little lounge chair to endure a seizure alone? What kind of father does that? Could it be, Dan, that Daniel's death is God's judgment upon you for your failure as a father?*

As we walked out of the hospital, those were exactly the kind of satanic thoughts that tormented me that day. The Evil One was indeed tempting me to think very hard thoughts about the Father and was leveraging against me my failures as an earthly father so that I was actually afraid to have good thoughts about my heavenly Father's love for me.[3] *Most certainly, Dan, your son's death is evidence of the Father's displeasure.* Knowing

3   Owen, *Communion with the Triune God,* 126–27.

well that I am battling with thoughts like those as I leave the hospital, Paul runs over, stops us in our tracks and says, "Dan and Melissa, come over here and sit down for a few minutes. I want to give you something really important."

As we sit down, Paul pulls out a pad of paper and begins to write exactly what my tormented heart so desperately needs to hear. After several minutes, he offers me his handwritten note:

Dear Dan,

Blessed be the God and Father of our Lord Jesus Christ, who has blessed you in Christ with every spiritual blessing in the heavenly places, even as he chose you in Christ before the world was created.

Never doubt that it was in the infinite warmth of his love that your Father adopted you as his dear child through Jesus Christ, and it was his will to purpose to do this. He wants you to know but also feel the glory of his grace in what he has done for you. He really wants you to marvel at the utter generosity of his love for you. So don't start doubting it now.

And don't ever think that he is indifferent to you or that he sometimes merely tolerates you. He has blessed you like this in his eternally beloved Son. And since you are in his eternally beloved Son, your Father can't do anything else but love you even as he loves his Son.

I know that you are likely feeling like you are being judged because of your failures. But never forget that in Christ you have the forgiveness of all your sins through his shed blood. There is therefore now no condemnation for you. None whatsoever. Not now. Not ever.

You are ever and always the Father's dearly loved son. Don't ever doubt this.

Your brother in Christ,

Paul

How comforting is that?

What I needed more than anything in the hours following my son's death was to hear the words of Ephesians' opening chapter, up close and personal, as if Paul had written them for me. As it turns out, he did.

True for you too

Of course, it can be difficult sometimes to accept that the good news of the gospel is meant for us personally, especially if we feel burdened by our past sins and failures. We may also feel like our past disqualifies us from receiving God's love and forgiveness. Shame or guilt about our sins can make it hard to believe that the gospel is actually meant for us.

But the gospel is not for those who seem to have it all together. It's for the broken, lost, and unworthy—for people like you and me. The good news is that God's love is not based on our performance or merit—it's a free gift available to all who believe. You are loved and accepted—because the Father loves to be gracious. So don't let your past hold you back from experiencing the fullness of God's grace.

The gospel is not a cautious announcement. It's not a hesitant word. It doesn't come with caveats. It never whispers, *Yes, you can be sure that the Father loves you—if, and only if, you love him with all your heart.* Really? No, the gospel is an extravagant word that is to be believed.

When Paul wrote Ephesians 1:3–14 to the church in Ephesus, he didn't want a single member to wonder if these words were actually written for him or her. He would not allow any Christian to say, "Yeah, but you don't know what I've done or what I've thought. You don't know my past."

So, lean into the truth of God's Word, for Ephesians chapter 1 does not give you a solitary reason to doubt what Paul says here about the Father's graciousness to you. As you read the announcement of the gospel *to you*, it is meant to be accepted without hesitation as good news for *you*.

Are you still finding it hard to accept this? Then imagine being in a Sunday worship service when the pastor pronounces a benediction over the congregation. In my tradition, raising his right hand, palms facing the people, he says, "The grace of the Lord Jesus Christ and the love of God and the fellowship of the Holy Spirit be with you all" (2 Cor. 13:14). "Go in peace."

Whenever that happens, I position my hands as if I'm about to receive a gift, which I am. I slightly raise them in front of me, palms upwards. This posture says, "I need what you are giving, and I gladly receive it." If the pastor is pronouncing those God-breathed words over me, he fully expects that I will receive them. And I do.

That's how you are expected to receive the good news of Ephesians 1: with open hands and a receptive heart. You have been given the grace to hear these God-breathed words of Paul, so open the "hands" of your heart. Take up and put on this belt of truth, the only belt that will keep you from stumbling under the assaults of the Evil One. Wear it because it is yours!

The gospel of peace

Come back with me, please, to Africa. The first stop of my flight home from Ethiopia was Khartoum, Sudan, and we passengers had to remain on the runway for the two-hour layover. So there I sat, knowing no one and totally alone with the darkness of my thoughts. Torment forced its way in like a conquering army so that I was completely robbed of peace. So deep had it invaded my heart, in fact, that I could not sense even the slightest sliver of the light of hope. Both light and hope seemed lost to me.

Attempting to distract myself by grabbing *People* magazine from the back of the seat in front, the first words I read, in large block letters, were: "HEATH LEDGER FOUND DEAD." So much for any chance of distraction. Torment laughed louder at me. My strength dried up.

Centuries earlier, Asaph had confessed, "But as for me, my feet had almost stumbled, my steps had nearly slipped" (Ps. 73:2). For me, it seemed there was no "almost" or "nearly." As far as I was concerned, my feet *had* stumbled, my steps *had* slipped. In those long hours, the battle for love appeared to be lost.

Have you ever found yourself in a place where darkness seemed to overwhelm you? Perhaps you too have felt the terrible weight of torment. The struggle for hope and light is one that we will all face at some point in our lives—if we haven't done so already. Some of us face this day in and day out.

It can be easy to seek distraction at such times, like I did by grabbing a magazine. However, in the midst of a storm, this type of "solution" can only do so much, for we need something more, something that can truly sustain us.

Enter Ephesians 6:15, where Paul writes, "... and, as shoes

for your feet, having put on the readiness given by the gospel of peace." Even as I reflect on that dark night of the soul, the words "the gospel of peace" fill me with a strengthening hope. Reading those words now feels like hearing Jesus say to me, "Get up, take up your bed, and walk" (John 5:8).

Speaking to people who once knew what it felt like to be utterly "separated … alienated … and strangers …, having no hope and without God in the world" (Eph. 2:12), Paul writes, "But now in Christ Jesus you who once were far off have been brought near by the blood of Christ. For he himself is our peace" (vv. 13–14). What does a separated and alienated people without hope in the world need? Answer: peace. And not an abstract or ethereal peace either, but peace that comes as a Person.

An enmity slain

Like an outdoor cat that brings its fresh kill to your front porch, the Evil One delights in bringing the bones of an enmity slain in ancient days to the door of your heart. Since he's well aware that you still sin and that you are certainly not what you should be, he knows how easy it is to get you to believe that your enmity against God still has a beating heart and flesh on its bones.

Stop for a moment and think about what that means. The Evil One bringing the bones of an ancient enmity to the door of our hearts is a vivid picture of how Satan tries to deceive us into thinking that God is still against us because our past sins and struggles still define us. It's a wicked yet effective tactic.

The torment I was feeling in Khartoum, Sudan, on that plane was an enmity that had already been slain (v. 16). I had lost sight of what Christ himself had done in his own body as he hung on the tree (1 Pet. 2:24). All of my enmity had been laid on him long ago, and he had borne it all, shedding his precious blood that he might bring me to God (1 Pet. 3:18). So complete was Christ's killing of my enmity as he suffered for me on the cross that he actually *became* my peace with the Father. This was the reality, whether I felt that peace or not.

So, the enmity no longer existed, yet still I felt its effects, like phantom pain from a long-amputated limb. Wrath, once deserved but now definitively dealt with, tormented me as if present. By contrast, the gospel of peace brought good news: Christ had already killed it through the cross (Eph. 2:16). Because of the sufficiency of Christ's shed blood, there was and is, now and forever, no condemnation for me (Rom. 8:1).

When you were separated from Christ, what you needed was for Christ to come to be your peace. And if now, as a Christian, you are tormented by the absence of peace, what you need is the fresh affirmation that *Christ himself is still your peace.* Since there is no more wrath for Christ because he has already extinguished the fire of wrath against your sin, there is no more wrath for you either. It's gone. Forever. And Jesus has already given you full access to the Father and brought you into the Father's household (Eph. 2:18–19).

Can you imagine a better pair of battle-tested "shoes" to wear when facing an enemy seeking to fill you with the dark doubts of despair and claiming that the Father can't possibly love you? If you are to withstand the opposition of cosmic forces, what you need is to be settled in your heart not only that your Father is never against you, but also that he is ever for you, even as he is ever for our Lord Jesus Christ. When the enemy seeks to trip you up in the dark night of doubt, the only shoes that will keep you on your feet are the "shoes" of the good news: Jesus himself is your peace with the Father.

The shield of faith

When I'm wrestling with doubts, my faith seems to be the main issue. *Maybe if it were just a bit stronger, I wouldn't doubt?* When I turn to Ephesians 6:16, which speaks of the next piece of armour, I read, "In all circumstances take up the shield of faith, with which you can extinguish all the flaming darts of the evil one." I'm puzzled. How can this "shield of faith" assist me in my battle? After all, isn't faith the root of my problem?

Whatever faith is and however we define it, Paul makes the value of the shield of faith immediately clear, for if you hope to extinguish the fiery arrows of the one who stands against you, then you must possess this shield. And to use it effectively, you must understand exactly what it is.

In Ephesians, Paul first mentioned the topic of faith with these words: "In [Christ] you also, when you heard the word of truth, the gospel of your salvation, and believed in him, were sealed with the promised Holy Spirit" (1:13). Remember that "the gospel," the good news, was the announcement of the Father's gracious love, made available to the Ephesians in Christ and giving them full and confident access to him (2:16, 18). This news was transformative, and the Ephesians embraced it eagerly.

So wonderful was this news, in fact, that it was also "made known to the rulers and authorities in the heavenly places" (3:10), which we learn are "the cosmic powers over this present darkness, ... the spiritual forces of evil in the heavenly places" (6:12). Paul adds these climactic words: "This was according to the eternal purpose that [the Father] has realized [or accomplished] in Christ Jesus our Lord, in whom we have boldness and access with confidence through our faith in him" (3:11–12).

The revelation that this news has been made known to the rulers and authorities in the heavenly places is truly awe-inspiring. Why? Because the message of God's love and grace is meant not just for our encouragement, but also so that the evil cosmic powers can know that what God has done means their days are already numbered. Yes, they remain our enemies, but they are defeated enemies.

You may feel like your struggles and challenges are insignificant in the grand scheme of things. But knowing that even the heavenly forces recognize the significance of God's love for you should fill you with comfort and hope. You are part of something much, much bigger than yourself! The fact that you have "boldness and access with confidence" through faith in Christ is a reminder that you can approach God with assurance and trust, knowing that his eternal purpose is being fulfilled in you.

When I feel discouraged and my faith seems weak, I sometimes read Theodore Tappert's *Luther: Letters of Spiritual Counsel*. Here we see how Luther often encourages struggling Christians to shout commands at the devil. He writes to a woman named Margaret who, after committing a sin, is being tormented by the thought that she belongs to the devil. To strengthen her faith, Luther writes:

He is a liar [and the father of lies]. Certainly it was not Christ who put into your mind the notion that you belong to the devil, for Christ died in order that those who belong to the devil may be released from his power. Therefore, do this: Spit on the devil and say: "Have I sinned? Well, I *have* sinned, and I am sorry. [But I shall not despair, for] Christ has taken away the sins of the whole world, of all who confess their sins. So it is certain that this sin of mine has also been taken away. Begone, devil, for I am absolved. This I am bound to believe. And if I had committed murder or adultery, or had even crucified Christ himself, this too would be forgiven if I repented and acknowledged the sin, as Christ said on the cross, 'Father, forgive them.'"

… Or [if you are still weak in your faith] say this: "I should like to be stronger in my faith, and I know very well that these things are true and to be believed. Although I do not believe them as I ought, yet I know that they are the [pure] truth." This is what it means to believe unto [righteousness and] salvation [as Christ says, "Blessed are they which do hunger and thirst after righteousness"].[4]

As I read Luther's advice to Margaret once again, it strikes me that he is encouraging her to repeat to the devil what God himself has already announced to him: *Look, Satan, my Son has accomplished complete forgiveness of her sins through his shed blood. There is nothing left for me to forgive. Therefore, I no longer hold anything against her. She is eternally forgiven, and I not only welcome her into my presence, but I also embrace her as my beloved child. You have absolutely no power over her anymore! Be gone!*

---

4   Theodore G. Tappert, ed., *Luther: Letters of Spiritual Counsel* (Philadelphia: Westminster Press, 1955), 102–103. Bracketed paraphrases original.

When Paul instructs you to take up the shield of faith to extinguish the fiery arrows of the Evil One, he is asking you to believe what God has already declared true about you to the devil. It is certain that the devil accepts God's declaration as true—he has no choice but to do so.

Do you ever feel like you're not good enough to approach God? Like you have to clean up your act before you can come to him? That couldn't be further from the truth! Ephesians 3:12 says that you have "boldness and access with confidence" to the Father through faith in Christ. It's like you're standing at the edge of a majestic cliff, looking out over the bluest and clearest ocean, knowing that you can jump into the Father's love and grace any time you want. He's already done everything that needed to be done. You were not involved. So, all that you need to "do" is hear the announcement of the Father's accomplishment for you and receive it.

The belt of truth, the gospel of peace, and the shield of faith are our weapons and our defence in the battle. Let's take a moment to bask in the good news of the gospel together. And let's keep gathering with our church family to hear and believe the amazing things that our faithful God has done for us.

3

OUR STRENGTH

"Dan and Melissa, this will be the hardest news you have ever heard, but you will need to give us permission to take your son off the ventilator. As horrible as this is to receive, he will not be leaving the hospital alive."

The words from our son's NICU doctor seemed to suck the oxygen out of my lungs. I vividly remember how I felt as that day moved heavily into evening.

It was Melissa's turn to spend the night in the NICU with Daniel. We would alternate three nights on, three nights off, and this was her third night. So, my parents drove me home. On the way, we stopped at a restaurant for a late supper so that I could eat my first real meal of the day. I sat in stunned silence, reeling from the news. *Our son would not leave the hospital alive.* As soon as we got home, I flopped down in a chair and let my head fall into my arms on my desk, sobbing uncontrollably. Devastation and helplessness were crushing me. My parents did the only thing they could do. Without saying a word, they knelt and wrapped their arms around my heaving body.

Another's strength

When I could no longer weep, the Holy Spirit reminded me of the words of Isaiah 53:4: "Surely he has borne our griefs and carried our sorrows." The thought that Jesus had borne all the overpowering grief and sorrow I was experiencing did something to me. Suddenly, I felt strengthened in my weakness. Now, that's not to say that I no longer felt weak, for I most certainly did. But another's strength began to uphold me even as I continued to feel overwhelmingly powerless. I still dreaded our son's approaching death, naturally, but now that dread was accompanied by the assuring strength of another in a way that surpassed my understanding.

Paul does not say to us in our weakness, "Just put one foot in front of another." If he did, then the emphasis would be on our action. Nor does he say, "God will not give you more than you can handle, so just keep pressing forward."

We know by now that we cannot find assurance of the Father's love by relying on, or looking at, ourselves, including our faith, love, and faithfulness. If we do, we are likely to experience more doubt than confidence, as there will always be holes—more and bigger holes—in our inner spiritual world. These holes or shortcomings are meant to encourage reliance not on ourselves, but on another and his strength.

Make no mistake: you may rightly be feeling utterly overwhelmed. At one point, Paul says that he and Timothy were so utterly burdened beyond their strength that they both "despaired of life itself" (2 Cor. 1:8). God certainly gave them more than they could handle, humanly speaking. It is not unusual to feel as if there is more difficulty in your life than you can possibly handle. The weight of responsibilities, the pressure of deadlines, and the stress of daily life can easily add up, leaving us feeling like we're drowning in our own problems. Sometimes it can feel like we're barely treading water, and then suddenly *wham!* An additional difficulty feels like it's pulling us under. At such times, we may feel like giving up or giving in.

So why does God allow us to face burdens that go beyond our capacity to bear? Paul writes, "Indeed, we felt that we had received the sentence of death. But that was to make us rely not on ourselves but on God who raises the dead" (v. 9). It is into that kind of context of weakness and powerlessness that Paul writes, "Finally, be strong in the Lord and in the strength of his might" (Eph. 6:10).

Paul's letter to the Ephesians is not a call to self-reliance but a call to Christ-dependence. Instead of insisting that you look inwards at your own faith and fruit, Ephesians lifts your eyes upwards and outwards to the faith and fruit of another. Paul's main objective is that you look outside yourself to the One who is your Lord, the One in whom you find the strength of assurance.

God gives you God

Paul knows that you cannot be assured of the Father's love in any other way than by being "strong in the Lord and in the strength of his might" (6:10). The Lord and his strength will enable you "to stand against the schemes of the devil" (v. 11). So, the power you need in the face of any paralyzing doubt is not found in new strategies or in a different approach or a better plan—you need a divine Person.

So, wonder of wonders, to empower you to fight against your devilish doubts, *God gives you God*.

Given the way God works, this makes perfect sense. Think of it logically for a moment. How did God deal with your greatest problem—namely, his wrath or anger against you in your sin?

First John 4:9–10 tells us:

> In this the love of God was made manifest among us, that God sent his only Son into the world, so that we might live through him. In this is love, not that we have loved God but that he loved us and sent his Son to be the propitiation for our sins.

"Propitiation" refers to the satisfying of God's wrath against us for our sins. There was no other way, such was the problem that sin represented. If God's wrath against you was your greatest problem, then only God could deal with it, because only God could fully satisfy his own anger. So, if God gives you God to meet your *greatest* need, should it surprise you, then, that he gives you himself in order to banish your doubts and suspicions too?

Loved indeed

Echoing the above, if there had ever been a time when the Father's heart was not filled to the full with love for you, wouldn't it have been when he was judging his Son for your sin? Yet it delighted the Lord to crush his Son when he bore your iniquities on the cross (Isa. 53:10).[1] Of this you can be certain: if the Father's heart was towards you in love when his Son bore your sin, it most certainly is towards you when you doubt his love. Apathy towards you or your doubts or struggles does not exist anywhere within God. Never is he *laissez-faire* about you, not even for a millisecond. His heart knows no cool detachment.

In fact, if you could look into the Father's heart and examine every last part of its infinite immensity, all you would see is love for you in your doubting condition. His heart is only ever coursing with love towards you as his dear child.

So, how is the Father's love revealed to you in the battle for love? As we saw in the previous chapter, the Father gave you his very armour (Eph. 6:11) so that you can be strong in the Lord Jesus Christ himself, with Christ's very own strength (v. 10). The Father's graciousness can be clearly seen by him giving you his very own strength in order to protect you. Now, that's love!

Be strong!

Paul uses three different words for power in order to stress the kind of divine strength God provides for you to stand confidently in the assurance of his love: "Finally, be *strong* in the Lord and in the *strength* of his *might*" (Eph. 6:10, emphasis added here and below).

And this isn't the first time he has used these three words in a single verse in Ephesians. Earlier, he prayed that the Ephesian believers would know "what is the immeasurable greatness

---

1   The ESV reads, "Yet it was the will of the LORD to crush him." The word translated "will" is a Hebrew verb meaning "to delight in." About this verse, Thomas Goodwin writes, "So much was his heart in our salvation, that this (otherwise the most abhorred act that was ever done) was sweetened to him by its end, our salvation, and made a matter of delight, not simply, but in relation to the end" (Thomas Goodwin, *The Works of Thomas Goodwin*, vol. 5 [repr., Grand Rapids, MI: Reformation Heritage Books, 2006], 286.).

of [the Father's] *power* toward us who believe, according to the working of his *great might*" (1:19). Those three italicized words—*power, great,* and *might*—are the same as in Ephesians 6:10.[2] And this is no coincidence, for Paul is telling us that this is the strength of God that we both need to know in our daily experience and utilize in our daily battle.

There is a vital connection here because the Father's threefold power towards those who believe is identical to a much greater one: the power "that [the Father] worked in Christ when he raised him from the dead and seated him at his right hand in the heavenly places, far above all rule and authority and power and dominion, and above every name that is named, not only in this age but also in the one to come" (1:20–21). Wow! That is reassuring indeed.

And Paul's emphasis on the Father's power would surely have been deeply encouraging to the Ephesian Christians. Having spent their entire lives as Gentile believers in Ephesus, a pagan city dominated by secretive religions oriented around the manipulation of spiritual power and magic, they had a strong tendency to fear that the gods of Ephesus were against them. According to their past understanding, these gods could be for you one minute and against you the next, for no apparent reason. Terribly fickle! Consequently, the believers had developed a deeply ingrained habit of attempting to keep the gods on their side by constantly trying to figure out what they needed to do to appease them. Doubt, suspicion, and fear became the order of the day. The Ephesians had no assurance that the gods

---

2   "Power" in 1:19 is the noun form of the verb "be strong" in 6:10, while "great might" in 1:19 and "strength of his might" in 6:10 translate words in each verse that share the same lexical root.

were for them or were inclined to show them any kindness or compassion.

It was into this cultural and religious context that Paul gave voice to his prayer affirming that the power the Father is "working" towards believers (v. 19) is the same as the power he "worked" when he raised Christ from the dead and seated him at his right hand (v. 20). For us today also, the power the Father employs towards believers is the same as that he employed towards Christ, with the same intention and outcome—namely, resurrection and exaltation (2:6).

I hope this encourages you as it does me. The words of Paul's prayer are a reminder of the transformative power of the good news of the gospel in the midst of a world marked by fear and uncertainty. Paul offers the Ephesian Christians, and us, a different way of understanding divine favour—it is not earned, but is a gift freely given by the Father to all of his children. You and me included!

What this means is that fear or uncertainty—even in the worst moments of our lives—are never sufficient cause to separate us from the love of God. When my son died, I felt as if I had been swallowed up by the deepest darkness, no longer able to feel God's comforting presence. For whatever reason, my experience went from knowing that God was with me in the days and hours leading up to my son's death to only feeling God's absence. My circumstances suddenly seemed to present an ironclad case that God was no longer for me. Both my son's death and the resulting emptiness within conspired against me.[3]

---

3   What I have not taken space to develop in this book is that physical and emotional exhaustion certainly contributed to this particular time of struggle for me. We are very

If—especially as you face trying circumstances—you find yourself doubting that the Father loves you or have a haunting suspicion that he merely tolerates you, Ephesians 1:19–20 beckons you to look at what the Father did for Jesus, precisely because it reveals what he's currently doing for you.

Remember the belt of truth, which keeps us from stumbling? When every hardship of our Lord's crucifixion and death seemed to conspire against him, the Father's almighty power was moving towards his Son to raise him from the dead and to seat him "at his right hand in the heavenly places" (v. 20). Never was the Father more for his Son than when circumstances were at their darkest. And that very same power is working towards all who cry out, "Lord, I believe; help my unbelief!" (see Mark 9:24), however dark things may seem.

Paul's prayer in Ephesians 1 reveals the Father's heart for his children and is a true gift from God himself. When we pray it, we can be certain that our Father is listening and answering, because our very words find their source in his loving heart. What's more, this prayer is a powerful reminder of the Father's plan for us. Just as he had a plan for his beloved Son in his darkest hours, so our Father has a plan for each one of us in ours.

Remember that, as inspired Scripture, this prayer was "breathed out by God" (2 Tim. 3:16). It naturally follows, then, that Paul prayed it because the Father wanted him to pray it, and God wanted Paul to pray it because he intended to grant the requests it contained. This God-inspired prayer reveals the Father's heart so that your heart and mine might be strengthened in the battle.

---

complex creatures, and it is good to take stock of our physical and emotional state whenever we are experiencing seasons of acute attack from within or without.

And remembering that God cannot lie must be our ultimate reassurance in times of doubt. Despite our desire for a multitude of reasons to believe in the Father's love, one simple truth should suffice, because of who God is and because of his very nature—yes, just one! Even if only a single sentence in Scripture affirmed that the Father loved us, that should be enough, for we read in Numbers 23:19: "God is not man, that he should lie, or a son of man, that he should change his mind. Has he said, and will he not do it? Or has he spoken, and will he not fulfill it?"

Given this, the statement that the Father "has blessed us in Christ with every spiritual blessing in the heavenly places" (Eph. 1:3) should be sufficient to convince us. Yet our natural inclination to seek more than what God has provided often leads us to doubt and convince ourselves that we require additional proof.

If you are feeling overwhelmed or uncertain, take comfort in this prayer. Our Father in heaven wants to silence our doubts and fears and replace them with the confidence that comes from knowing we are loved and cherished by him.

Strengthened *in the Lord*

God has promised so much. Some form of "in Christ" or "in him" or "through Christ" appears ten times in Ephesians 1:3–14: everything the Father has done for you was done in or through Christ. Every last drop of blessing the Father has ever promised to bless you with is found "in Christ." All is yours already, in him.

If you have ever had the opportunity to visit Niagara Falls, you will know that one of the most thrilling experiences is standing on Hurricane Deck at the Cave of the Winds. Located at the base of the Niagara Gorge, this wooden deck sits just a few feet from where the water from the falls cascades down. To get there, you take an elevator that goes 175 feet down through the solid rock and then make your way along the wooden walkways that bring you to the Deck.

As you approach, the sound of the rushing water becomes louder and more powerful until it is all you can hear. The wooden boards beneath your feet begin to shake as the water crashes against the rocks below. You can see the mist rising from the falls and feel the wind growing stronger as you get closer. With around 750,000 gallons of water plunging over the falls every second, the sheer force of the water is truly awe-inspiring.

Once you step onto Hurricane Deck, you are completely surrounded by the powerful force of the water as it hurtles down just a few feet away. The mist is so thick that you feel as though you are standing in a heavy rainstorm, and the wind is so strong that it can be difficult to keep your footing. It's intense.

Now, imagine someone standing on Hurricane Deck, terribly thirsty from a long day in the sun, and deciding to try to drink Niagara's cool water. Head up, mouth open, he wants to consume every last drop. As he drinks, he suddenly thinks, "You know, I should probably stop drinking so that there will be enough water for other thirsty tourists." If Niagara could overhear that man's thoughts, it would laugh mockingly at him: "Who are you to think that you can even begin to deplete my supply?"

But what if there *were* a man who could stand under Niagara and enjoy every last drop of its endless supply of water? That would be beyond astonishing. And yet the sheer number of the Father's blessings infinitely dwarf the amount of water that has ever flowed, or ever will flow, over Niagara, and Jesus contains them all. So, like the man drinking from Niagara, you stand "in Christ" and are free to enjoy every last drop of the Father's blessings.

It shouldn't surprise you, then, that Paul concludes Ephesians by encouraging you to be strong *in the Lord*. It's true that, on our own, we don't have sufficient strength. When it comes to receiving and enjoying all that the Father has done for you, *in the Lord* is key. We don't find the strength to face our doubts within ourselves, but by relying on One who is far greater.

We'll now turn to the firm foundations and fortifications that we do well to examine and call to mind in the tough times if we are really to embrace the truth that we are *loved indeed*.

PART 2

Our Foundations and Fortifications

4

PURE LOVE AND ROCK-SOLID SECURITY

My earthly father was a remarkable parent who consistently demonstrated an immense personal and loving interest in me as his son. I have fond memories of him sacrificing his evenings to drive me to a local basketball court after sunset. He even aimed our car's headlights at the basketball goal to ensure that I could see, and then he would rebound hundreds of shots for me. I always felt my father's love for me, but I also recognized the obvious: that when he was working, teaching music theory at the local college, he couldn't think of me at the same time. Being a mere human, his finite nature limited the extent and ability of his thoughts. Though this didn't mean he loved me any less, it did mean that there were natural limitations on how and when he would express his love.

In stark contrast, your heavenly Father's thoughts of you and me know no limits. They are boundless in time and eternity. And ever since the Father's thoughts have been set upon his eternal Son, he has lovingly set them upon you too (Eph. 1:4–5).

Now, I realize that not everyone has had the privilege of growing up with a loving and attentive father. For those of you who may have experienced neglect, abuse, or absence at the hands of your earthly father, the idea of a father's love can evoke painful memories. And even those who have a very loving and supportive earthly father may struggle to believe that their heavenly Father loves them. This struggle is not a respecter of family dynamics.

Your heavenly Father is not like *any* earthly father. His thoughts towards you are infinite and everlasting, and his love for you is perfect and unwavering. No matter what your earthly father may have done, or failed to do, you can find enduring comfort and security in the boundless love of your heavenly Father.

If the eternal nature of your Father's thoughts towards you is true, and it is, then how attentive do you believe he is to you and your needs right now? Jesus says, "Are not two sparrows sold for a penny? And not one of them will fall to the ground apart from your Father. But even the hairs of your head are all numbered. Fear not, therefore" (Matt. 10:29–31).

Have you ever tried to count the number of hairs on your head? On average, we lose 50 to 100 hairs per day, making it nearly impossible to keep track of the exact number. Jesus is conveying here that your Father is far more attentive to you than even you are to yourself.

Although you may think about yourself more than any other person does, your thoughts are like a single drop of water compared with your Father's thoughts of you. Whatever your status or perceived importance in the world, he values and cherishes you. Your Father sees and cares for you in a way that far exceeds your imagination and comprehension. And as we saw earlier, his every thought is firmly rooted in his love for you from "before the foundation of the world" (Eph. 1:4).

Don't fear the unknown

The unknown can be terrifying. One summer, I found myself sitting in a 220-lb. kayak, a mile offshore in the Atlantic Ocean. Although 220 pounds may seem very heavy for a kayak, and a mile not a great distance, I can attest to the fact that when something brushes against the underside of your ocean-floating kayak, your vessel feels incredibly light, and the distance from shore suddenly seems much farther. The vast and untamable nature of the ocean can easily make us imagine the worst-case scenario as we contemplate floating atop the great depths of the unknown.

Relating to God can feel that way to us too. Just as an infinite amount of coffee cannot be contained within a 12-ounce mug, there is so much more to know about the infinite God than our tiny, finite minds can hold. And since God is far beyond our searching and taming, the Evil One seeks to exploit our fear of the unknown. As we know all too well by now, he works tirelessly to make us fear God as our avenging judge rather than run to him as our loving Father.

But although we finite creatures may not be able to fully comprehend God, we must remember that we can undoubtedly still _know_ him, and know him well. Scripture contains all that we need for a profound sense of security in the face of all that we do not know about him. And Paul gives us a vital glimpse into eternity past to help us understand an unknown aspect of

God: he reminds us that the Father "chose us in [Christ] before the foundation of the world" (Eph. 1:4).

The unknown corridors of eternity may indeed scare us. I recently had a conversation with a man who was troubled by the fact that God chose (or "elected")[1] his people before anything existed. He had realized for the first time that he might not like the teaching of Scripture on election. And he was afraid, because he felt he could not know if he was among the chosen or not. The idea that his eternal destiny was entirely out of his control terrified him, and he worried that he could end up being a child of wrath after all (Eph. 2:3).

Is this something that has troubled you? The way we view election has a lot to do with what we believe about the heart of God. The devil wants us to believe that under the infinite and unknown depths of God lie the leviathans of his wrath, ready to consume us. However, Paul reminds us that when it comes to these fathomless depths, there is only love—a love that is eager to comfort us and provide us with the security we need to handle the great unknown. So, in light of this, Paul's words in Ephesians 1:4 should encourage rather than terrify us—in the same way that hearing those words as written to *me* (as shown in my "letter" from Paul in the hospital lobby earlier) helps me rest in God, relying on him without fear.

God's loving intention

So how do Paul's words inspire confidence that election is good

---

1   The doctrine of election is the belief that before the foundation of the world, God chose certain individuals to be saved through faith in Jesus Christ. This choice was not based on any merit or goodness in the individuals themselves, but solely on God's gracious will and purpose. Those who are elect are irresistibly drawn to faith in Christ and preserved by God's grace until the end.

and not bad news? What reasons do you have to believe that the Father loves you and will continue to do so for all eternity?

My wife and I know something about adoption. In 2001 and 2003, we adopted our sons Isaiah and Noah. From the time when we were told that their birth mothers had selected us to be their parents, all of our love and energy was focused on adopting them.

But one major difference between my love for my sons and the Father's love for you and me is that my love has a definite "before" and "after." At a specific point in time, my love for them as unique individuals began. Before they were born, I did not know them, so it was only after their birth mothers chose us that I could set my love upon them. For my sons, everything about my love for them hinged on a particular moment in time.

The Father's love for you, however, is eternal and unchanging, with no "before" and no "after." God "predestined us for adoption … as sons" (Eph. 1:5), so even before time began, the Father had the sovereign intention of adopting you. Never for a moment was this not his loving plan. Paul wants you to be fully assured: the Father has indeed chosen you from before the foundation of the world and predestined you for adoption. Remember, his sole purpose in Ephesians 1:4–5 is to encourage and reassure you of the Father's glorious grace so that you may offer praise to him.

The Puritan pastor Thomas Goodwin expresses this sentiment quaintly but eloquently: "God hath been your ancient friend, even from everlasting … God hath been thy Friend and Father from everlasting, therefore forsake him not; *he hath loved thee ever since he loved himself* … He is such a friend as never had his thoughts off from us. There is not a moment in which he hath not loved us, and had his thoughts upon us."[2]

A love not based on merit

Earlier, we saw how the Ephesians lived in constant fear before they believed in Christ. Their relationships with the pagan gods were entirely based on merit: if you did what the gods wanted, assuming you could somehow figure out what that was, then they might decide to be kind and bless you. *Might.* There was never any assurance, and therefore never any confidence.

Instead of gods who are hard to please, Paul reveals a Father whose choice is not dependent on your merits and efforts at all, for his choosing you eternally preceded the first beat of your heart in your mother's womb. And since God chose you before you even existed—and in spite of fully knowing the ocean of sin you would one day commit in thought, word, and deed—there is nothing for you to figure out. There is nothing to *do*: you can't earn his love, because he already gave it. The Father loves you simply because he loves you. By locating the Father's decision to bless believers in eternity past, Paul flips the script.

If you are like me (and I think you know me well enough by now to tell), you can read the above paragraph and *still* stress about your complete lack of merit. *But you don't know what I've done!* And yet, into our angst, 2 Timothy 1:9 speaks and assures us that the Father saved us "not because of our works, but because of his own purpose and grace, which he gave us in Christ Jesus before the ages began."

So, be reassured. There was no reluctance whatsoever on the Father's part to choose you, no uncertainty. The Father was not

---

2   Thomas Goodwin, *The Works of Thomas Goodwin*, vol. 7 (repr., Grand Rapids, MI: Reformation Heritage Books, 2006), 192, emphasis added.

forced, nor was there any sense of obligation or indifference. Rather, he *desired* to choose you.

No distant father

Your Father in heaven doesn't just want a house full of children. Nor is he merely providing room and board until you're ready to move out on your own. He hasn't "delivered us from the domain of darkness and transferred us to the kingdom of his beloved Son" (Col. 1:13) to provide us only with safety and sustenance, as wonderful as those are.

Few words fill my heart with more wonder and warmth than the final words of this statement: "[The Father] predestined us for adoption to himself as sons" (Eph. 1:5). The Father's sovereign intention in adopting you was to bring you *to himself* in order to give you *himself*. Here is no distant father.

We noted earlier how "the belt of truth" (6:14) points back to "the word of truth" (1:13), the gospel of your salvation. And every molecule of that good news is fully animated with the Father's innumerable thoughts towards you from all eternity (1:4–5). Our Father fully intends that the meaning of "to himself" should wash over you like cool water on a scorching day. And as it does so, this glorious truth will refresh and renew your mind and heart, strengthening you in your battle against the devil's evil schemes. Writing eloquently of the Father's thoughts of you, David says, "How precious to me are your thoughts, O God! How vast is the sum of them! If I would count them, they are more than the sand" (Ps. 139:17–18). Grains of sand—think about it!

When it was time for us to adopt our sons, I had to move towards them. Naturally. For Isaiah, this involved travelling from

Greenville, South Carolina, to Lexington, Kentucky, about a five-and-a-half-hour drive. For Noah, it was to Florence, South Carolina, just under three hours away. In both cases, I had to go to where they were in order to bring them to where I lived. And crucially, that whole process from home to them was fuelled by love.

The Father's home, by contrast, is "the heavenly places" or heavenlies (Eph. 1:3). Here the Father, in the words of Jonathan Edwards,

> is manifested and shines forth in full glory, in beams of love. And there this glorious fountain forever flows forth in streams, yea, in rivers of love and delight, and these rivers swell, as it were, to an ocean of love, in which souls of the ransomed may bathe with the sweetest enjoyment, and their hearts, as it were, be deluged with love![3]

So when Paul says that the Father predestined you for adoption to himself, he meant bringing you to the heavenly places, where love overflows. And to be in the heavenlies is to be secure, impossibly so, in the Father's love.

We saw in the previous chapter how the Father's love for you is beyond comprehension: he went to extraordinary lengths to bring you to himself, sending his Son from his home of perfect love to enter our world of sin and death and descend into the grave (4:9). Through Christ's sacrificial death, the Father extended grace and mercy to you, adopting you as his beloved child. Before Christ intervened, you were trapped, dead in

---

3   Jonathan Edwards, *Heaven Is a World of Love* (Wheaton, IL: Crossway, 2020), 37–38.

your sins, and following the ways of the world (2:1–3). But the Father's love could not be stopped, so he moved towards you in Christ. His grace was so abundant that Christ willingly descended into death to pay for your forgiveness (1:7). This descent is the very expression of the Father's love for you.

T. F. Torrance served as a stretcher-bearer on the front lines during World War II before his academic career in theology. On one occasion, he came upon a mortally wounded soldier who was dying but still conscious. As the blood poured, the soldier looked up, terrified, into Torrance's eyes and asked, "Padre, is God really like Jesus?"[4]

In other words: "I can believe that Jesus loves me because he died for me, but can I believe that the Father loves me too?" When facing the inevitability of his impending death, the wounded soldier desperately wanted to know if he could trust the Father's love.[5]

The love of the Son and the love of the Father are one and the same. The love of the Son expressed through his sin-bearing death for you is indeed the revelation of the Father's love for you from all eternity. Crucially, Christ's love *is* the Father's love for you, unleashed in the world in order to bring you to himself.

Risen and ascended for you

Isn't it amazing what Christ accomplished on your behalf? Through his death on the cross, he paid the price for your

---

4   Cited in Alister McGrath, *T. F. Torrance: An Intellectual Biography* (London: T&T Clark International, 2006), 74.

5   Paragraph adapted from *Reclaiming Adoption: Missional Living through the Rediscovery of Abba Father,* ed. Dan Cruver (Minneapolis, MN: Cruciform Press, 2011), 37–38.

forgiveness. And then, in a stunning display of his almighty power, the Father raised him from the dead and exalted him to his right hand in the heavenly realm (1:20).

Can you fathom the depth of the Father's love, not only poured out in this world but also triumphing over death itself? Indeed, Jesus was brought to the Father's own presence, seated at his right hand, where he now intercedes for you. Such comforting and reassuring truths for us to hold on to!

Do you remember my story in the Introduction? If we are not careful, we can read statements like those in the previous paragraph and think, "That's all well and good for Christ. I'm thrilled that the Father brought Christ to himself, that he's secure at the Father's right hand. But I'm the one who needs assurance. I'm desperate for a sense of security that can extinguish all the flaming darts of the Evil One. I am the one who actually needs good news."

"Hold on," says Paul. Immediately after talking about your condition before you first believed in Christ (2:1–3), he continues,

> But God, being rich in mercy, because of the great love with which he loved us, even when we were dead in our trespasses, made us alive together with Christ—by grace you have been saved—and raised us up with him and seated us with him in the heavenly places in Christ Jesus, so that in the coming ages he might show the immeasurable riches of his grace in kindness toward us in Christ Jesus. (2:4–7)

The Father brought *you* to himself by bringing Christ to

himself. The Son did not become man for himself—he was conceived by the Spirit in the virgin womb of Mary *for you* (Matt. 1:21–23; Luke 1:35). What Christ did for you as the Representative Man is your security. So, in a nutshell: Christ became man *for you*. Christ died *for you*. Christ rose from the dead *for you*. And he ascended to the Father *for you*.

In the Old Testament, David poses the question, "O LORD, who shall sojourn in your tent? Who shall dwell on your holy hill?" (Ps. 15:1). Then he answers,

> He who walks blamelessly and does what is right and speaks truth in his heart; who does not slander with his tongue and does no evil to his neighbor, nor takes up a reproach against his friend; in whose eyes a vile person is despised, but who honors those who fear the LORD; who swears to his own hurt and does not change; who does not put out his money at interest and does not take a bribe against the innocent. He who does these things shall never be moved. (vv. 2–5)

I used to read this and feel unsettled and insecure. David's words would turn my gaze inwards, and, looking at what was in my heart, I was reminded that I was certainly not blameless. Unnerved, I would ask, "What right do I have to dwell in the heavenly places at the Father's right hand?"

But David does not leave us there. The very next verses (Ps. 16:1–2) calm the doubting heart: "Preserve me, O God, for in you I take refuge. I say to the LORD, 'You are my Lord; I have no good apart from you.'" We take refuge in the Lord precisely because without him we cannot enjoy the benefit of "fullness of joy" and "pleasures forevermore" at the Father's right hand (v. 11).

No refuge, no security can be found within us. It's only to be found in the man Christ Jesus (1 Tim. 2:5).

So whenever you are plagued by the serpent's poison of doubt, look on the One who was not only lifted up on the cross for you (John 3:14–15), but who also ascended to the Father's right hand with you.

In him alone, you and I are secure forever.

5

ANCHORED IN LOVE

You've heard the saying: "Out of sight, out of mind." Well, I seem to be one of those people who struggles with that reality more than others do. At least, it seems that way to me.

I wish this struggle weren't an issue for me. If I am not regularly around people, I can go for weeks without thinking about them. It really doesn't matter who it is either. (I am a little embarrassed to give you any examples at this point, so I won't!) So to compensate, what I normally do is provide myself with frequent prompts to think about individuals, often using an app like iCalendar on my phone. If I don't, then it's likely I'll neglect even relationships that are very important to me.

At times, theologians throughout church history have referred to the Holy Spirit as the neglected person of the Trinity, often overshadowed by the Father and the Son. I think the neglect (or overlooking) may be partially due to the Spirit's primary purpose of pointing us towards Christ instead of drawing attention to himself. If I can put it this way, the Spirit usually stays out of sight as he works, which means he's often out of our minds too.

What's unfortunate (and ironic) about this is that the Spirit plays a vital role in strengthening our assurance. As we established in previous chapters, the Father and the Son both want us to live each day with confident assurance that we are theirs. But it's not as if the Father and Son care about our assurance while the Spirit can take it or leave it. It's not as if the Father cares about bringing many sons and daughters into his family while the Son and the Spirit don't. The beauty of God being one is that each person of the Godhead cares about the same things. Because the three persons of the Trinity are the one true God, they each care equally about everything that God cares about. There is only one caring, and it's the caring of the one God. And this includes care for your sense of assurance.

Objective versus subjective

When I find myself thinking about the Spirit, my mind usually goes to what he does within me subjectively. *Am I feeling God's presence? Am I experiencing love, joy, peace, patience, kindness, and goodness today? Am I feeling convicted about my sin?*

However, to draw a parallel, consider the concept of familial relationships: whether we are adopted or are natural-born children of our parents, being their "children" isn't something we have to actively "feel" all the time in order for it to be true. If someone asks us, "Are you x's son or daughter?", we don't consult our internal experience to confirm this. Our status as their child is true objectively, regardless of whether we "feel" like it at a particular moment in time. Similarly, we are God's children positionally, and it's not practical to always be verifying if we "feel" that way as a primary check of its truth.

For the Christian who struggles with assurance due to an inclination toward introspection or in the midst of extremely difficult life circumstances, it's essential to remember that our hope and confidence rest not on our subjective experiences, even if they are the work of the Holy Spirit, but on his objective presence within us. The Spirit is always indwelling us objectively, even when we are subjectively unaware of his activity.

The objective work of the Spirit is as much hidden from our experience as the Father's objective election of us in eternity past. But the Spirit's hidden work is just as important to our assurance as the Father's choosing of us.

Sharing in the divine life

As a Christian, you are called not just to trust in God, but, amazingly, to know him intimately and personally as a loving Father who invites you to share in the triune divine life. Towards the end of Jesus' High Priestly Prayer, John 17:24–26 offers a beautiful picture of the loving communion between the Father and the Son, and of how it extends to believers who have been given to Christ by the Father.

Jesus says to the Father, "Father, I desire that they also, whom you have given me, may be with me where I am, to see my glory that you have given me because you loved me before the foundation of the world" (John 17:24). Jesus' desire to be with his people in his glory is rooted in the eternal love that flows between the Father and him. It is *this* love that is the ultimate ground of our assurance as Christians, for it is the unbreakable eternal love between Father and Son that guaranteed our placement as children within the family of God before we even existed. And our sharing in this divine love cannot be deserved or merited (as discussed above), and because of that, God will not withhold it from you. Ever. God chose you out of grace alone.

If you find yourself protesting, "But Jesus only prays that we would see his glory. It says nothing about us sharing in it," then you are to be commended for taking the wording of Scripture very seriously. Fortunately for us, Jesus' prayer continues: "I made known to them your name, and I will continue to make it known, that the love with which you have loved me may be in them, and I in them" (v. 26).

So, through the kindness of Jesus, we are welcomed into knowing the Father's name and experiencing the warmth of his love. That same love, shared between Father and Son from all eternity, is now something we are to experience too.

Everlasting union

Jesus didn't just promise this assurance but made a divine commitment to ensure it happened. And he did this by sending someone like him—a Comforter—after he left. In those quiet moments before he journeyed to the cross, Jesus comforted his disciples by saying, "I will ask the Father, and he will give you another Helper, to be with you forever, even the Spirit of truth … . You know him, for he dwells with you and will be in you" (John 14:16–17). Even in those tense hours before his death, Jesus wasn't going to leave his friends feeling abandoned.

Jesus gave his disciples a promise that wouldn't fail. "I will not leave you as orphans," he said (v. 18), painting a picture of heartfelt reunion. Even as he prepared to say goodbye, Jesus was actually getting ready to say "hello" again.

Jesus' promise wasn't just about sending some distant figure or vague impersonal power to be with his disciples, but rather the Spirit of truth, the third person of the Trinity—a companion who commits to be with them forever, dwelling within them in a deeply personal and unending union.

A love that cannot be shaken

As we step back to reflect on this beautiful reality, we may find ourselves wanting a better understanding of how the persons of the Trinity actually relate to one another. To help guide us through this profound mystery, let's lean on the wisdom of a trusted elder in the faith.

Meet Augustine of Hippo, a theologian from the fourth century whose thoughts have been lighting the way for the church for centuries.

As we've just seen in John 17, Scripture shows us the Father's love for the Son and the Son's love for the Father. But it may not be as obvious how the Spirit fits in. This is where Augustine will be our guide. He tells us to think of the Father as the one who loves the Son, the Son as the one whom the Father loves, and the Spirit as the love they share. This helps us understand what Paul said in Romans 5:5: "God's love has been poured into our hearts through the Holy Spirit who has been given to us."

According to Augustine, the Holy Spirit isn't just the means the Father uses to pour his love into our hearts—like you'd use a jug to pour iced tea into a glass. And it's not like there are separate actions—one for the Father to pour his love into our hearts and another for the Spirit to live in us. No, when the Spirit lives in you, even if you don't feel his presence, you are filled with the same love that the Father and the Son share. If the Spirit lives in you, you carry within you the love of the Father and the Son that has been there forever. In this way, you are held steady in a love that cannot be shaken or taken away.

Swept up into boundless love

In chapter 1, I introduced a brief exploration of adoption in the rich opening verses of Ephesians (1:3–14). By beginning his letter with this focus on the Father's infinite love for us, Paul displays his intention that we should live confidently in God's love, as opposed to falling prey to doubts stirred up by our enemy. In chapter 4, we deepened our understanding of divine adoption by comparing it with human adoption in order to illustrate the Father's unchanging and eternal love: unlike human love that has a beginning, God's love preexists our lives, and it doesn't depend on our merits. The core theme was God's unceasing intention to bring us to himself in the heavenly places through the sacrificial death and triumphant resurrection of his Son, Jesus Christ.

But what is the Spirit's role in our experience of adoption? You may be feeling a bit of tension here. "Yes," you agree, "the Spirit does objectively indwell us as Christians whether we feel his presence or not. But certainly, there must also be times when we experience the Spirit's presence subjectively, right? Shouldn't our hearts be aware of his presence from time to time?"

Paul seems to anticipate questions like these in his letter to the Galatians when he writes,

But when the fullness of time had come, God sent forth his Son, born of woman, born under the law, to redeem those who were under the law, so that we might receive adoption as sons. And because you are sons, God has sent the Spirit of his Son into our hearts, crying, "Abba! Father!" (Gal. 4:4–6)

What a treasure trove of truth Paul offers in these verses! When he speaks of the Father sending his Son, "born of woman," he is inviting us to fix our gaze upon an objective event, one of unchanging significance regardless of what is going on with our emotions. And then he highlights the objective accomplishment of the Son as a man: redemption so that we might become the Father's children through adoption. Once again, God does something that's not at all dependent upon our perception of it. And then comes one of my most cherished verses in all of Scripture—one that speaks of the warmth of the Father's love.

Pause for a moment and reflect upon this beautiful sequence of divine grace. First, the Father sent forth his beloved Son to accomplish our redemption, and then, after his Son victoriously fulfilled his mission, the Father sent his Son's Spirit to take up residence in the very depths of our hearts.

Here's where Paul takes us by the hand, gently leading us from the objective to the subjective, to give us a sense of assurance that's very tangible—the Spirit actually does something within us that can be felt. Whenever you cry to God as Father, you can be sure that the Spirit is subjectively at work in you.

Can you see the beauty of how Paul connects the objective with the subjective, and all for your benefit? As the Spirit—the personal bond of love between the Father and the Son—dwells objectively within you, one of his primary works is to lovingly cry out, "Abba! Father!" in the inner sanctuary of your heart.

His presence within you signifies an astounding reality: you have been swept up into the boundless love of the Trinity.

Our guarantee

In a world plagued by uncertainty and doubt, this assurance becomes our anchor, securing us in the unchanging love and promise of God. Paul's words in Galatians 4 fill our hearts with deep and lasting confidence in our relationship with the Father.

When assurance and security can feel like distant stars far beyond our grasp, Paul's simple words in Ephesians 1:14 bring them closer to us. Paul tells us that the Spirit is the very "guarantee of our inheritance." This concept of making a "down payment"[1] is one we are familiar with when making significant purchases like a house or a car, signifying our investment, our willingness, to put our own resources on the line. But when Paul presents the Spirit as a down payment, he is taking this analogy to a whole new and breathtaking level.

Picture this: Paul is suggesting that the very Spirit who is the bond of love shared by the Father and the Son is himself God's down payment for us. Let that sink in. Paul is expanding this analogy in a way that should astonish us.

As Paul endeavours to unpack the "secret and hidden wisdom of God" (1 Cor. 2:7) for the Corinthian church, he paints a stunning portrait: the Spirit is the one who searches the depths of all things, even the mysteries of God. What a staggering thought! Solomon, in all his wisdom, acknowledged that even the "heaven and the highest heaven cannot contain" God (1 Kings 8:27). Yet, this uncontainable, infinite God is fully known

---

[1] The Christian Standard Bible reads, "The Holy Spirit is the down payment of our inheritance."

by the Spirit—because the Spirit is himself God.

When Paul declares that the Spirit is your down payment, your guarantee, he doesn't mean that the Spirit is merely a portion of the whole. He actually means to encourage you with something incomprehensibly grand. It's as if your down payment surpasses the full expanse of the universe! When the Spirit takes up residence within you, you receive something more—infinitely more—than the entire universe. The Spirit is your sure guarantee.

As you meditate on this truth, allow yourself to be drawn into greater awe and praise for the vastness of the Father's love for you.

Father!

From 2008 to 2015, I had the privilege of leading the nonprofit organization Together for Adoption. This gave me the humbling opportunity of visiting orphanages around the world, from China and Ethiopia to Haiti and South Africa.

One particular visit remains etched in my memory. I entered an orphanage housing three hundred children, all aged three or younger, with two-thirds of them under the age of one. Sadly, the place was severely understaffed, with just one worker for every twenty-four children. In a room filled with sixty cribs (and most held two infants), only four workers were available to tend to their needs. Despite these individuals' tireless efforts, they struggled to provide adequate care. It was at that moment that I viscerally encountered the cry of the orphan. Sometimes their cries were loud and filled with anger. At other times, they were deafening in their silence.

Have you ever experienced such intense grief that you

couldn't utter a sound? If so, or if you have heard the cry of the orphan in your own life, you will know exactly what I am talking about.

During such times in my life, my heart—though my voice was silent—could only cry one word in desperate longing: "Father!" Even when the intensity of the experience subsided enough for me to catch my breath, the only prayer that escaped my lips was the repeated cry, "Father!" On many occasions, I have found myself sitting on the edge of my bed, head in hands, my heart simply echoing, "Father! Father! Father!"

Do you know what's truly happening in those moments? It's the Spirit, faithfully carrying out the work described in Galatians 4:6, assuring me that I am firmly anchored in the boundless love of the triune God. It is the Spirit, sent by the Father and the Son, crying within the depths of my being and testifying to the reality of my adoption into God's family.

In your moments of overwhelming grief or despair, when words fail you and your soul feels burdened beyond measure, take comfort in the truth that the Spirit is at work within you. He is the seal, the down payment, the guarantee of your eternal inheritance. He cries out from the depths of your heart, uniting your voice with the unending chorus of all God's beloved children, declaring, "Abba! Father!" It is in these profound encounters with the Spirit's presence that we find solace, reassurance, and hope, even amid our darkest storms. It is here that the objective and subjective aspects come together.

Let the deep and abiding assurance of God's love and presence be your strength. Remember that you are anchored in the very love of our triune God. Let the cry "Father!" be your refuge and strength, your comfort and peace, knowing that our triune God—Father, Son, and Holy Spirit—has claimed you as his own. In this assurance, you will discover the unwavering embrace of the Father, the transforming power of the Son, and the abiding presence of the Spirit, guiding you through every season of life. Rest in the depths of love, for you are eternally cherished by the God who calls you his own.

6

TEN LOOKS AT CHRIST

Just weeks ago, after forty-one hours of labour, my daughter Hannah gave birth to our first grandchild. She worked hard to fix her eyes on the goal of those labour pains, but this was extremely difficult to do. Her mind was fixed on the pain she had to endure with each contraction. Yet the moment she laid her eyes on her baby boy, that one look filled her with a joy she had never before experienced. Pain gave way to joy (John 16:21).

The wise Scottish pastor Robert Murray M'Cheyne memorably wrote, "Learn much of the Lord Jesus. *For every look at yourself, take ten looks at Christ.* He is altogether lovely. Such infinite majesty, and yet such meekness and grace, and all for sinners, even the chief! Live much in the smiles of God. Bask in his beams. Feel his all-seeing eye settled on you in love, and repose in his almighty arms" (emphasis added).[1]

We have focussed much on the doubt and suspicion within

---

1   Andrew Bonar, *Memoir and Remains of the Rev. Robert Murray M'Cheyne* (Edinburgh: Banner of Truth, 1966), 293.

us. Now it's time to "take ten looks at Christ." Why? Because he is altogether lovely. To see his loveliness is to banish all doubt.

So, let's gaze at ten portraits of the beauty of Christ[2] so that you will "repose in his almighty arms," both while you read this book and long after you have set it down. I focus especially on death at the end because if we see Jesus as our comfort amid all the threats of death, then every other fear will begin to pale into insignificance. Several portraits touch on some of what we have already covered by way of reminder, while others are fresh looks at who Jesus is for you.

Your Father's heart

Stepping back a generation from the story above, when Melissa was three months into her pregnancy with Hannah, I started writing letters to the daughter whom I had yet to meet. Each morning, I'd write a short note in a journal, sharing my love as her father and my desire that she would come to know the heavenly Father and Jesus Christ (John 17:3). This practice continued even after her birth, and expanded in due course to my other children too. Today, Hannah, Isaiah, and Noah—now grown-up—can open these journals and read years' worth of letters that reveal my heart for them.

The purpose of my letters was to express my deep love and longing for my children. However, for all of us, Jesus provides an even clearer window into love. He goes beyond mere words, directly revealing the Father's heart for us. For instance, in Mark

---

2   Of course, there are more that we could consider. The walls of eternity will be covered with portraits of Christ that will take our breath away. But for now, ten are enough. One idea I suggest is that once you finish reading this book, you grab a journal or notebook to record other "looks" at Christ not covered here. For instance, you could look at portraits of Christ presented in Ephesians and Colossians, or 1 Peter and 1 John, or the Gospel of John, or indeed in any other book of the Bible.

10, we find the disciples turning away parents who are bringing their children to Jesus (vv. 13–16). But when Jesus sees this, he rebukes them: "Let the children come to me; do not hinder them, for to such belongs the kingdom of God" (v. 14).

Note how Jesus' heart was drawn to little children. Jesus was the kind of Saviour who loved children and wanted them to experience his tenderness towards them, his compassion for them. He was eager for them to know that he would enjoy spending time with them. He was never in a hurry to move on to more "important" things.

Our Father in heaven has revealed his heart for us by speaking his decisive word to us by his Son (Heb. 1:1–2), who is the "exact imprint of his nature" (v. 3). So, the Father's love, intentions, desires, and heart are perfectly revealed in Jesus. If you want to know the Father's heart, then look no further than Christ. He is the very embodiment of the Father's love for you.

Jesus himself said, "Whoever has seen me has seen the Father" (John 14:9). So, in short, Jesus is not just the one who *knows* the Father; he's also the one who *shows* the Father. And this means that when we witness Jesus' tender care for children, of which my numerous letters to my own children are only a tiny picture, we're getting a glimpse into the Father's heart of boundless love for each one of us. Amid whatever turbulent circumstances you may be going through, Christ reveals that you are eternally held securely in your Father's arms, the subject of his unhurried joy and delight.

So, look at your heavenly Father and know that you are *loved indeed.*

Your Saviour's beauty

To look at Jesus' physical appearance when he walked this earth was to see a man who was neither impressive nor handsome. When the prophet Isaiah predicted the arrival of the incarnate Son, he wrote, "For he grew up before him like a young plant, and like a root out of dry ground; he had no form or majesty that we should look at him, and no beauty that we should desire him" (53:2). Nothing about the way Jesus looked would have drawn your gaze or admiration. His looks weren't the kind to inspire envy or admiration. No one looked at Jesus and thought, "Oh, I sure wish I looked like him."

Jesus' loveliness was not found in his physical features, but rather expressed in what he did for us. Isaiah added, "Surely he has borne our griefs and carried our sorrows; yet we esteemed him stricken, smitten by God, and afflicted. But he was pierced for our transgressions; he was crushed for our iniquities; upon him was the chastisement that brought us peace, and with his wounds we are healed" (vv. 4–5).

Christ's labour of love, his complete surrender, and his suffering for us carried within them a beauty that far eclipses the most awe-inspiring display of a million sunsets. Christ, who for all eternity past had been the very shining forth of divine beauty in all its fulness, willingly embraced our ghastly burdens of sin, grief, and sorrow. In his suffering, he painted the masterpiece of redemption, not with strokes of visible appeal, but with brushes dipped in his own selfless love and blood-stained sacrifice. In him, "Beauty" truly loved the "beast," becoming sin for us "so that in him we might become the righteousness of God" (2 Cor. 5:21).

By the same token, as you gaze at Christ, know that his

love for you is not dependent on your physical attributes, your achievements, or even your personal faithfulness. It flows entirely from his own divine nature. For just as he was unremarkable in appearance yet accomplished the extraordinary task of redemption, so too he loves you not for your remarkable traits but simply because he is your Saviour and you are his child. He bore the deepest pains and took on the darkest sins—not of the virtuous or the strong, but of all who are broken and weak.

Whenever you feel insignificant, remember that the world's estimation of value is different from Christ's. His beauty is found not in the heights of earthly beauty, but in the depth of his sacrifice, and in that sacrifice you are profoundly cherished. He doesn't just love the idea of you—he loves the real you, with all your scars, flaws, and failures. His love is steadfast, and it won't let you go. Let his wounds be your healing and his love be your assurance today.

Beauty matters hugely in our world. But whoever you are and whatever others think, you are *loved indeed* by One whose beauty transcends all other beauty.

Your Brother's ascension

If you want to know whether or not morning has come, you look outside at the sky. Similarly, if you want to be certain that God is for you and not against you, look outside yourself to Christ, seated at the Father's right hand. As we reflected earlier, Christ's ascension into the Father's presence is really good news for you. Why? Everything that needed to be dealt with was fully and entirely dealt with *before* Christ took his seat. He did not sit down "at the right hand of the Majesty on high" until *after* he made purification for your sins (Heb. 1:3). This means

God never deals with you according to your sin (Ps. 103:10), whether it's past, present, or future, and no matter how big it might be. The enduring presence of Christ within the Father's love is your eternal confidence that God is always for you, never against you.

Look outside! Only by looking at the ascended Christ can you know you are *loved indeed.*

Your guiding Light

Have you ever travelled to a city for the first time and arrived there at night? In one sense, you are seeing the city, but there is so much more of it that you are *not* seeing. As a result, your understanding remains incomplete; certain parts are concealed under darkness, hiding potential dangers. It is not until you go out the next morning that you begin to see the city for what it really is.

Jesus said, "I am the light of the world. Whoever follows me will not walk in darkness, but will have the light of life" (John 8:12). Yet when Jesus went to the cross, it appeared that the Father had forsaken him, that he was against him. And if he was against the perfectly holy and righteous Jesus, then how could we ever have any confidence that he is not against us too?

But when Jesus, the Light of the world, was raised from the dead, he said to Mary Magdalene,

> "Do not cling to me, for I have not yet ascended to the Father; but go to my brothers and say to them, 'I am ascending to *my Father and your Father, to my God and your God.'*" Mary Magdalene went and announced to the disciples, "I have seen the Lord"—and that he had said

these things to her. (John 20:17–18, emphasis added)

With those words, Jesus assures us that because of what he did for us at the cross, his Father is always our Father. There is no hidden Mr. Hyde in him. To look at Jesus, to trust him, is to know that the Father only ever treats you as his child.

"God is light, and in him is no darkness at all" (1 John 1:5). You are *loved indeed* by One who is the light and who will always lead his followers in light.

Your empathetic Forerunner

Although Christ is now in heaven (Heb. 4:14), he is not an unfeeling mediator, detached from your human condition of weakness. Rather, he was tempted as you are "in every respect," but never once did he sin (v. 15). Only someone who has endured more temptation than you have, and did so without sinning, is able to provide the help you need.

Temptation did its best, pressing him, trying to push him beyond the very limits of his humanity. And yet he endured, "becoming obedient to the point of death, even death on a cross" (Phil. 2:8). He did not run from his weakness as he endured temptation after temptation to turn from the path of obedience.

The good news of the gospel is that in spite of Jesus' human frailty, he always did what pleased the Father—because, frankly, you and I haven't done so (John 8:29).

Because Jesus was obedient unto death on our behalf, he loves to meet us in our weakness. He never looks upon us with apathy, disdain, or indifference when we come for help. Rather, he is touched by our plight and frailties. And because of this, he

TEN LOOKS AT CHRIST

offers a throne of grace, not one of judgment. He invites us to come boldly in time of need (Heb. 4:16).

Our Forerunner empathizes with us. We don't have to run and hide, but instead we run into his loving and welcoming embrace.

Your place in the family

Hebrews 2:11 says something quite amazing: Jesus is not ashamed to call us his brothers or sisters. Think about that. Jesus, God's own Son, the second person of the eternal Trinity, is proud to call us—people who continue to sin and fail to follow—his family.

This means that Jesus, who in his divinity is higher than the highest heavens and whose glory is beyond human comprehension, willingly identifies with those whom he sanctifies. And he identifies with you as the one who is your sanctification, your righteousness, and your future glorification (1 Cor. 1:30; Heb. 2:10).

Christ is not some distant, impersonal deity, but a close and loving brother who identifies intimately with you, even to the point of being proud to call you family. So great is his love, so complete is his work of redemption, that he will forever claim you as a sibling that he delights in. And you can be sure that there is no sibling rivalry whatsoever with Jesus.

Your perfect Intercessor

We who follow Christ often find ourselves facing seasons of doubt in prayer. *Is the Father truly listening?* we may wonder. Here's where, once again, the beautiful relationship between Jesus and the Father should eliminate our concerns. Jesus, having walked among us as a man, knows our struggles, our fears, and our deepest desires (Heb. 4:15). But as God, whenever he prayed, Jesus knew the Father was listening to every word he uttered. And since as man, he was also our Great High Priest, he wasn't speaking to the Father just for himself, but for you.

Imagine your prayerful words, hopes, and dreams being taken, perfectly purified, and presented to the Father. That's what Jesus does for you. In fact, Hebrews 7:25 says that "he always lives to make intercession" for you. As Jesus prays on your behalf, he brings your human experiences to the throne of grace, ensuring that the Father always hears and understands you. And it isn't just about words. When Jesus intercedes, he puts his whole self into it, standing in for you, advocating for your needs and desires. And since he himself is the one true God, his prayers perfectly align with the Father's desires for you: Jesus' desires and the Father's desires are the same. So, every single prayer of your High Priest is met with a loving and enthusiastic "yes."

In Jesus, you have one who carries your words, your feelings, straight to the Father. So the next time you pray, remember this: through Jesus, you have the Father's undivided attention. He listens, he cares, and he answers. With Jesus, your confidence in prayer can be unwavering.

Keep looking to your perfect Intercessor.

Your Worship Leader

When we worship as the gathered church, this especially is the time and place for us to "take refuge in the shadow of [God's] wings" (Ps. 36:7) so that we can "feast on the abundance of [his] house" and be given "drink from the river of [his] delights" (v.

8). Yet there are many times when we doubt our worthiness even to worship God.

What should we do when we need to worship but don't feel worthy to do so? Your High Priest, "who is seated at the right hand of the throne of the Majesty in heaven" (Heb. 8:1) never leaves you on your own to worship the Father. He never abandons you in the Father's presence. *Never.* Jesus is always there to purify every last bit of your weak and frail attempts to worship, and he always offers your worship as "holy and acceptable" (Rom. 12:1) to the Father for you. In short, Jesus sits at the Father's right hand as your permanent worship Leader (Heb. 8:2).[3]

The truth is that we can't offer acceptable worship to God on our own. Never once in your life, in your own strength, have you offered acceptable worship to God! But don't worry, for that's what Jesus does for you as your Great High Priest. Hebrews 2:12 puts the words of Psalm 22:22 onto the lips of Jesus precisely because he's the only one who can offer worship that the Father accepts: "I will tell of your name to my brothers; in the midst of the congregation I will sing your praise." As your worship Leader, Jesus takes your frail, imperfect worship—even and especially when your heart feels empty and desperate for God's joy—and presents it, now perfected in him, to the Father on your behalf.

Since Jesus enables your worship, every time you gather as a

---

3   According to James Torrance, "The writer of the Epistle to the Hebrews describes our Lord as the *Leitourgos* (Heb 8:2): 'the leader of our worship,' 'the minister of the real sanctuary which the Lord pitched and not man.' As such, the *leitourgia* of Jesus is contrasted with the *leitourgia* of men and women. This is the worship which God has provided for humanity, and which alone is acceptable to God" (*Worship, Community & the Triune God of Grace*, 16). We get our word "liturgy" from the Greek word "*leitourgos.*" Thus, Jesus is our worship Leader.

church, you can fully expect the Father to nourish you from his abundance and quench your thirst from his river of delights. And yet Jesus doesn't just do this when you gather at church. He purifies your every attempt to offer yourself to the Father "as a living sacrifice" (Rom. 12:1).

So, go on. Offer away this very second! Jesus turns your every gift of worship into "a fragrant offering, a sacrifice acceptable and pleasing to God" (Phil. 4:18).

What a wonderful High Priest you have!

Your certain future

The letter I received was from an elderly Christian woman. Her fear of death, once a distant thought but now preoccupying her, was causing great angst. Her faith, usually a source of comfort, was becoming overshadowed by fear, and she felt like she was treading unknown waters, alone and far away from the loving reassurance of God.

How did I respond? I reminded her that the Father's love for her is revealed by the very Person who "upholds the universe by the word of his power" (Heb. 1:3). He doesn't merely hold the universe's molecules together: the Greek verb translated "upholds" implies leading or carrying everything into the future ordained by the Father. So, Christ personally moves the course of history—her personal story included—towards its appointed destination. From the moment the eternal Son was conceived in Mary's womb, he didn't merely promise her a glorious future, but he actively began carrying that dear woman's very life towards her God-ordained destiny.

Death is a condition inherent to our fallen human nature. But as we know by this point, the Father's Word to us, his Son, chose to share in our humanity. The almighty God, in the likeness of our humanity (Heb. 2:14), journeyed through the valley of the shadow of death because of our sin. His death was a victory, a shattering of the chains that bound us to the fear of death (vv. 15–16).

In a world where death can seem to loom around every corner, we might be tempted to despair. But Christ did not promise us a life without suffering, a path without hardship, or an escape from the experience of physical death. But he did promise us his presence, his sympathy, and his victory. He is not just a Saviour who saves us from afar, but our Brother who has already walked through the valley of death *for* us. He intimately knows your pains, your fears, and your struggles, and has already carried them to the cross.

Let his victory be your peace, and his love your comfort. Because Christ has already conquered death, you are freed from its fear. He is your hope for eternal life.

Rest in this glorious truth today and all the days of your life. As you confront any fears and uncertainties about the future, know that Christ will not fail to give you what he has promised.

He is faithful, and will be faithful to the end.

Our unshakeable kingdom

Just before Christmas in 2020, my parents contracted COVID-19. And on January 4 and 6, 2021, only forty-eight hours apart, they passed away.[4] Our family's world was rocked from top to bottom.

---

4   I discuss this in slightly more detail in the Appendix.

In this shakeable, fallen world, death is our final enemy (1 Cor. 15:26). All the pain, sorrow, and tragedy we fear is a testament to this world's shakeable nature: everything is impermanent and fleeting. Yet while we face many enemies in our lives, none is as relentless and inescapable as death. It casts a looming shadow over human existence, constantly reminding us of our fragility and the transient nature of life in a world tainted by sin. Death stands as the Mount Everest towering over every other shakeable mountain in our fallen world. Against this bleak backdrop, Christ holds you absolutely secure.

A day is coming when God will shake the created order one final time (Heb. 12:26–27). And when God shakes both the heavens and the earth, this will not be a time of chaos or destruction, but a transformative act, removing all that is part of this fallen and corrupted creation. When Christ shakes all things shakeable, he won't be dealing with your sin—for he's already done so once for all time—but rescuing you from every effect of the fall (Heb. 9:28). In that day, Christ will eradicate even your final enemy, death, erasing it entirely from his renewed creation. In the unshakeable kingdom he ushers in, death will be a distant memory, replaced by eternal life. Sorrow, pain, and mortality have no place. If that is what Christ will do one future day, you can be sure that he will rescue you from death's grip when it breaks into your life today or any other day.

When death comes knocking, Christ will personally rescue you from it because he entered into it (Heb. 2:9), was buried, and was then raised to an indestructible life (7:16). And he did all of this for you (2:14–18).

Oh, how you are loved by Christ—more than you can possibly imagine. He is your hope of indestructible life. Do not fear.

You will not be shaken on the day of your death, but instead will be served by the Lord Christ himself.

My friend, you are *loved indeed.* Don't ever forget it.

A LOVED AND LOVING MAN: ADMIRING A CHRISTIAN FATHER

Here is an example of what your life can look like when you live with assurance of the Father's love for you. My prayer for you and for me is that our triune God will continue to do in our lives what he did in my father's (and mother's).[1]

My father died of COVID-19 on January 4, 2021. My mother died of COVID-19 just forty-eight hours and three minutes later. At the time, losing both parents within two days of each other felt like far more than I could take.

The depth of the grief and shock that my brothers and I felt was compounded because, due to heightened regulations during the pandemic, we could not visit Mom in person, but had to tell her of Dad's death over FaceTime. It was the most

---

1   A version of this account under the same title was published at desiringGod.org on June 19, 2022.

difficult conversation I have ever had, and we are fairly certain that the devastating news of her husband's death contributed significantly to Mom dying so soon afterwards. Having been separated for a week by two hospital floors, she lost the man who loved her most without ever getting the opportunity to say goodbye.

I share the circumstances of my parents' deaths because I believe they highlight the kind of man and husband my father was.

In health and in sickness

For nearly fifty-six years, my father loved my mother with a fierce, self-sacrificing love—in health and in sickness.

My mother was seriously ill for well over half of their marriage. When I was fifteen, she was only days away from dying from ulcerated colitis, which she had battled for several years. If it had not been for God putting her in the hospital that had the only surgeon in the country who was capable of doing this particular type of life-saving surgery, she would have died.

In those many months of suffering, I witnessed my father lovingly care for Mom when the pain was so severe that the only relief she could imagine was to die and be with the Lord. He was a full-time music professor during the week and our church's music minister on Sundays. And he was always a very present father for his three sons. My father's care for my mother was daily marked by a love I could observe but not fathom.

In 1999, my mother was diagnosed with stage 4 ovarian cancer. Once again, her suffering was intense, and Dad's care was remarkable. My wife and I were teachers at the time, and we were off for the summer, so we decided to take the nine-hour drive to live with them for a month. Oh, what a month it was. Dad's loving care for my mother in her sickness remained indomitable. He loved; I marvelled.

And in humility

Lest my reflections above tempt you to think that my father didn't struggle with temptation and sin, I'd like to tell you about something that has impacted me even more than his love for my mother. I actually believe it holds the key to understanding how he loved the way he did.

Throughout the entirety of my growing-up years, from elementary through high school, if my father realized he had sinned against me (or my brothers), he would come and say something like, "Daniel [or one of my brothers], I was wrong to do/say that. Would you please forgive me for sinning against you?" My father never merely apologized. If he thought that he had sinned against me, he asked me for forgiveness.

Every time my father did that, my admiration and respect for him grew. Here is a man, I thought, who walks in humility before God and others. Even more than his fierce love for my mother, my father's asking his sons for forgiveness has impacted and shaped me, mainly because of what it revealed to me about his God.

"Skies of parchment made"

My father was a consummate musician. I remember him telling us boys of the time when Stan Kenton, the king of big bands in the 1940s and '50s, recruited him to play trumpet. For all the love my father had for jazz, though, he loved sacred music even more.

For decades, my father taught music in Christian colleges, and while he did that, he would also lead worship on Sundays at our church. My mother would play the piano while he directed the choir and led corporate worship.

This was back in the days when churches would have "special music" in the worship service. Over the many years I heard my father sing solos, the song that left the deepest impression upon me (and I probably heard him sing it over twenty times) was "The Love of God" by Frederick M. Lehman:

The love of God is greater far
Than tongue or pen can ever tell.
It goes beyond the highest star
And reaches to the lowest hell.
The guilty pair, bowed down with care,
God gave his Son to win;
His erring child he reconciled
And pardoned from his sin.

Could we with ink the ocean fill,
And were the skies of parchment made;
Were every stalk on earth a quill,
And every man a scribe by trade;
To write the love of God above
Would drain the ocean dry;
Nor could the scroll contain the whole,
Though stretched from sky to sky.[2]

---

2   Frederick M. Lehman, "The Love of God" (1917), stanzas 1 and 3. Lyrics in the public domain.

Every time he sang it, my heart would burn within me. This was the song that revealed what made my father's heart tick. He was a man who saw the love of the Father written large, and he couldn't get over it. Whenever he sang of the Father's love, you knew he was singing "to the praise of [the Father's] glorious grace" (Eph. 1:6).

Fuel of his love

Often when I think of my father, my mind goes to Luke 7, where we read of the sinful woman who shed tears on Jesus' feet. She "wiped them with the hair of her head and kissed his feet and anointed them with the ointment" that she brought with her (v. 38).

When confronted by a Pharisee for letting a sinful woman touch him, Jesus said to him, "I tell you, her sins, which are many, are forgiven—for she loved much" (v. 47). Jesus is not saying that the woman was forgiven because she loved much. No, he was saying that the evidence she was forgiven was that she loved much.

If we say, "Summer has come, for the temperature has reached 100 degrees," we do not mean that summer has come because of the high temperature. We mean that the evidence of the arrival of summer is the scorching heat. Or, to say it a different way, the effect of summer is 100-degree weather. My father's love for my mother and the humility needed to ask me for forgiveness were the evidence and effect of the Father's great love for him, by which he was forgiven of all his sins. He loved much because he had been forgiven much.

What more could a son want?

Over the many decades that I watched my father care for my mother, God the Father graciously gave me a regular glimpse of something of what it meant for Christ to love the church and give himself up for her (see Eph. 5:25). My father loved my mother like he did because he couldn't get over how Christ had loved him.

But that kind of love wasn't limited to my mother; it spilled over into how he loved his sons—into how he loved me. My father was kind to me, tenderhearted, forgiving me and humbling himself to ask for my forgiveness, because God in Christ had forgiven him (see Eph. 4:32). He was unwaveringly humble because he knew just how much mercy he had received in Christ.

As I look back on my father's life, it is clear to me that he was carried by love—not by a love of his own making, but by the love of the Father in Christ Jesus, poured into his heart through the Holy Spirit (Rom. 5:5).

Oh, how I miss him! In my eyes, his life was "lived to the praise of the Father's glorious grace." What more could a son want?

SCRIPTURE INDEX

Help us see reformation today

By giving regularly, **Friends of Union** help make our ministry of growing leaders and growing churches possible. Will you join them?

BECOME A FRIEND OF UNION TODAY

Go Deeper with Union

Discover books, articles and free resources to help you delight in God,
grow in Christ, and serve his church at **unionpublishing.org**

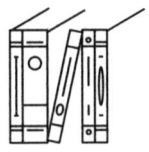

Find more books and
resources to help you
delight in Christ at
unionpublishing.org

UP

GIVEAWAY

RECEIVE FREE
RESOURCES EVERY
MONTH WHEN YOU
SUBSCRIBE TO
UNION PUBLISHING.

UP

Union

DELIGHTING IN THE TRINITY

WITH MICHAEL REEVES